Cambridge Elements$^{\equiv}$

Elements in Contentious Politics
edited by
David S. Meyer
University of California, Irvine
Suzanne Staggenborg
University of Pittsburgh

RELATION-BUILDING AND CONTAINED RADICALIZATION IN THE GAZA PULLOUT CAMPAIGN

Eitan Y. Alimi
The Hebrew University of Jerusalem

CAMBRIDGE
UNIVERSITY PRESS

Shaftesbury Road, Cambridge CB2 8EA, United Kingdom

One Liberty Plaza, 20th Floor, New York, NY 10006, USA

477 Williamstown Road, Port Melbourne, VIC 3207, Australia

314–321, 3rd Floor, Plot 3, Splendor Forum, Jasola District Centre,
New Delhi – 110025, India

103 Penang Road, #05–06/07, Visioncrest Commercial, Singapore 238467

Cambridge University Press is part of Cambridge University Press & Assessment,
a department of the University of Cambridge.

We share the University's mission to contribute to society through the pursuit of
education, learning and research at the highest international levels of excellence.

www.cambridge.org
Information on this title: www.cambridge.org/9781009511896

DOI: 10.1017/9781009511933

When citing this work, please include a reference to the DOI 10.1017/9781009511933

First published 2024

A catalogue record for this publication is available from the British Library.

ISBN 978-1-009-51189-6 Hardback
ISBN 978-1-009-51190-2 Paperback
ISSN 2633-3570 (online)
ISSN 2633-3562 (print)

Relation-Building and Contained Radicalization in the Gaza Pullout Campaign

Elements in Contentious Politics

DOI: 10.1017/9781009511933
First published online: November 2024

Eitan Y. Alimi
The Hebrew University of Jerusalem

Author for correspondence: Eitan Y. Alimi, eitan.alimi@mail.huji.ac.il

Abstract: This Element explores the Jewish Settlement Movement's campaign against the Gaza Pullout as a case of contained radicalization. Despite the presence of militant worldviews and propensities for aggression, as factors identified in the literature as drivers of political violence, the campaign saw little violence. The Element offers a detailed analysis of the history of relation-building within the movement and between it and the Israeli State and its agents to explain the ability of leaders from the various contending parties to contain radicalization. It traces the emergence and evolution of central relational mechanisms operating within and between the contending parties over time and during past campaigns. By demonstrating the effects of these mechanisms during the campaign against the Gaza Pullout, the Element shows how the mutually reinforcing relational dynamics mitigated the salience of aggressive propensities and violence-prone ideologies, consequently putting a brake on radicalization.

Keywords: radicalization, relation-building, Israel–Palestine, Jewish settlers, Gaza Pullout

ISBNs: 9781009511896 (HB), 9781009511902 (PB), 9781009511933 (OC)
ISSNs: 2633-3570 (online), 2633-3562 (print)

Contents

1 Introduction

On July 19, 2005, approximately one month before the implementation of the Israeli government's plan for disengagement from the Gaza Strip, a massive gathering of Israeli protesters and security forces confronted each other in an agitated standstill outside the Strip. On one side, tens of thousands of activists and supporters of the Settlement Movement arrived at the scene as part of what they called the "connection march" with the declared intention of breaking into the quarantined Gaza Strip. On the other was an unprecedented force of eighteen thousand armed police and soldiers with the unequivocal governmental directive to defend the quarantined zone at all costs and prevent protesters from infiltrating the Gaza Strip settlements. The tense atmosphere was exacerbated by wide-spread media coverage and by public opinion, partly informed by Israeli General Secret Service evaluations, claiming that the chances of civil war were high. Revealingly, however, the aggrieved mass of protesters quietly turned back after a highly charged exchange between leaders of both sides. The protesters marched into a nearby small town, surrounded by a heavy police force. It took several days of picketing, public prayers, vigils, and provocative attempts to break through the town's fences before the protesters eventually complied with the police order to leave the site.

The "connection march" was the height of an almost eighteen-month-long campaign against the government's disengagement plan, also known as the Gaza Pullout. In early 2004, amidst the ferocious second Palestinian Intifada and as part of a controversial unilateral policy concerning the Occupied Territories,[1] Prime Minister Ariel Sharon made the Plan public (see Figure 1). It was not the first time Sharon had raised the possibility of engaging in painful compromises over territories. Nonetheless, the publicity given to the Plan in early 2004 after an interview with the Israeli daily *Ha'aretz* and the degree of specificity with which Sharon presented it made the gravity of the moment clear. The plan entailed the evacuation of more than 9,000 Israeli citizens from all twenty-one Gaza Strip settlements and an additional four settlements in the upper part of the West Bank.

The smaller of the two Palestinian territories occupied by Israel in the June 1967 War (the other being the West Bank), the Gaza Strip differed in several important aspects. Politically and geographically, located along the southern coastline of Israel, it was controlled by Egypt. In contrast, the West Bank was under Jordanian rule and located inland along the center of Israel. Demographically, the Palestinian

---

[1] The term Occupied Territories refers to the Gaza Strip, the West Bank (inclusive of East Jerusalem, renamed Judea and Samaria shortly following the June 1967 War), the Golan Heights, and the Sinai Peninsula.

The Green Line
Municipal boundaries of Jerusalem after 1967
Palestinian town/village (built-up areas)
Jewish settlement in the West Bank (built-up areas)
North Samaria
Gaza Strip
Jewish settlements evacuated in 2005

Figure 1 Map of disengagement plan, 2005

Source: Shaul Arieli's Israeli-Palestinian Conflict Maps Archive

population of the Gaza Strip was less spread out and was mainly centered in three exceptionally high-density areas: in the north of the Strip, around the city of Gaza; in the center, around the town of Deir al-Balah; and in the south, around the city of Khan Yunis.

Israel's takeover of these areas in 1967 saw two main developments: The first was the use of measures meant to prevent Palestinian residents from returning to their homes after the war ended, to force them out of the country, or to lure them to do so via a variety of incentives (Segev 2005). The second was Jewish colonization following a governmental decision in June 1970, and was carried out as part of a larger program called the Five Fingers Plan. The idea was to establish army footholds throughout the Gaza Strip in order to divide the Strip at five different horizontal lines from north to south. Israel established the first army foothold in October 1970, which became the precursor of the bloc of agricultural villages later to be known as Gush Katif (Hebrew for harvest bloc). While the first colonies were not necessarily religious in affinity, nor did they occupy a central role in the Settlement Movement, the situation gradually changed over the years as a result of economic, security, and political developments (Admoni 1992; Pedatzur 1996; Huberman 2005).

Alarmed by the unprecedented scope and volume of the Pullout, Jewish settler and right-wing organizations that were part of the broader Settlement Movement launched what became the most intensive, wide-ranging, and sustained cycle of contention in the history of Israel: the anti-Pullout campaign. Relying on an unprecedented pool of resources and allies within the political establishment and the general public, the movement mobilized hundreds of thousands of activists and supporters in various institutional and extra-institutional orchestrated contentious events. Between February 2004 and August 2005, movement actors initiated legislative motions, votes of no-confidence, street rallies, mass marches, vigils, and countrywide barricades and traffic jams. They even managed to bring about ministerial resignations and a vote on a public referendum bill for the first time in the history of the Israeli Parliament (the Knesset).

Despite noteworthy achievements, the anti-Pullout campaign failed to stop the implementation of the plan. Between August 15, 2005, and September 22, 2005, Israeli security forces ended the almost four-decade-long Jewish presence in the Gaza Strip – organized in settlements, most in the Gush Katif bloc – dismantling as well four settlements located in the northern part of the West Bank. The campaign was highly intense and tumultuous, involving numerous acts of disruption and passive resistance, but was largely nonviolent. Throughout the campaign (and the actual weeks of eviction, for that matter), only a handful of violent incidents aimed against Israeli and Palestinian targets occurred (see Figure 2 below). Some of these violent incidents were not directly related to the pending Pullout; others involved self-harm or were initiated by individuals with no organizational affiliation.[2]

---

[2] This assertion is based on a systematic collection of data on contentious events and the coding of violent events according to whether or not an event resulted in bodily or property damage. All data presented in this Element follow the same coding rules. Treating instances of passive resistance and other disruptive acts as violence, no matter how drastic and threatening they were, would be a gross over-stretch. Including foiled attempts or uncovered plots would be problematic as well, as it conflates different criteria. Though the campaign did involve such events, they were coded as disruption or classified them as intentions (i.e., militant incitement to violence – see Figure 2 below).

1.1 The Context

The full significance of the predominantly nonviolent nature of the struggle against the Gaza Pullout should be evaluated in light of the rich record of engagement in political violence (including terrorist violence) by member factions and groups of the broader settlement movement.[3] Taking shape following the June 1967 War and aiming to settle the territories occupied by Israel after the war, the movement ultimately became the most influential social movement the State of Israel has ever known (Newman 1985; Lustick 1988; Sprinzak 1991; Pedahzur 2012; Hirsch-Hoefler and Mudde 2020).

While settlement attempts had begun shortly after the 1967 War, a full-fledged settlement campaign started only after the October 1973 Yom Kippur War. Alarmed by the territorial withdrawals associated with the armistice agreements with Syria, Egypt, and Jordan, a group of activists formed the Bloc of the Faithful (Gush Emunim) and embarked upon a determined drive to settle Samaria, the northern part of the West Bank. Their relentless campaign to establish a settlement near Sebastia, a Palestinian village located in the West Bank, north of Nablus, lasted from June 1974 until December 1975, and involved eight settlement operations before a compromise with the government was reached.

The Sebastia campaign exemplified several features of the movement that combine to present the tension between two strains of political activism that has kept shifting in one of two directions ever since – one toward militancy and radicalism and the other toward moderation and pragmatism. First, an inherent tension existed between movement actors' commitment to the law of the State (i.e., *Mamlakha* – Hebrew for kingdom) and Jewish law (*Halakha*), often expressed in valuing religious principles and injunctions over those of the State's legal system. At times, this tension extended to two opposing approaches vis-à-vis state institutions and Israeli democracy more broadly, namely *Mamlakhtiyut* (i.e., an integrationist approach) versus *anti-Mamlakhtiyut* (i.e., a segregationist approach) (Lustick 1988; Peleg 2002). Second, seeking to act as a bridge between secular Zionist Israelis and Ultraorthodox Jews and claiming to represent the entire Jewish-Israeli public, the movement nonetheless systematically aimed at catering to the Religious-Zionist[4] public sector. Promoting a separate educational system, youth clubs, and special army units often led to tense relationships between religious and secular elements within the movement and a hostile stance toward Israeli progressive forces

---

[3] In this Element, the term *settler* has a different meaning from *colonist*. A settler is a person seeking to colonize a particular land or territory they believe was promised to them by a divine power, in this case, the God of Israel.

[4] An ideology and a "camp" (or grouping) within the Zionist Movement and, post-independence, within Israeli politics and society. Religious Zionism views Zionism and Jewish nationalism more broadly as a fundamental component of Orthodox Judaism rather than as an anti-thesis of it.

(Dalsheim 2011). Finally, due to the settlement population's broadening presence inside the Occupied Territories and daily friction with the Palestinian population, the relationship between it and Israeli security forces was frequently tenuous. The tension between normative and instrumental stances among movement actors toward Israel's defense forces became particularly acute during heightened Palestinian unrest and upheaval. Alongside compliance, cooperation, and at times collusion with the defense forces, were also growing signs of vigilantism and willingness to raise arms against soldiers and police officers (Weisburd 1989; Levy 2007; Gazit 2015)

Whenever the government endorsed a policy restricting settlement activity or considered territorial compromises, the movement experienced intense internal factionalism and, at times, the splintering away of radical factions engaging in violent actions against Palestinian and Israeli targets. Some examples were the formation of a clandestine network called the Jewish Underground during the implementation stages of the Camp David Accords between Israel and Egypt, which initiated attacks against Palestinian targets; the Sicarii underground group active during the first Palestinian Intifada, which carried out a terrorist campaign against Israeli leftwing intellectuals; and, later, a small underground group formed by Yigal Amir and his brother, which was responsible for assassinating Prime Minister Rabin in late 1995 in the context of the Oslo Accords.

Without underestimating the importance and gravity of these (and other) challenges, the Gaza Pullout plan was unprecedented in its adverse conse-quences for the settler community and the settlement enterprise. It was the first time the Israeli government had evacuated a predominantly religious settler population of such a magnitude and from so many settlements – all located in territories many Israeli Jews considered to be an integral part of the biblical promised land of Israel (i.e., Greater Israel). Moreover, the plan was announced amidst the ferocious second Palestinian Intifada and was seen by many as the continuation of a highly controversial and submissive unilateral policy toward the Occupied Territories (i.e., the construction of a separation barrier). Finally, the anti-Pullout campaign witnessed constant Palestinian attacks on settlements, increasingly vocal Israeli opposition groups, and escalation of incitement to violence by ultra-radical settler groups. Public polls and assessments by security advisors and specialists reported in the Israeli press offered dark predictions of a civil war. As it turned out, however, there was little violence in the anti-Pullout campaign.

This Element's account of why there was little violence during the anti-Pullout campaign represents an attempt to add something meaningful to our understanding of a highly recurring and pertinent phenomenon: *Radicalization*.

Radicalization is commonly defined as the systematic, frequent adoption of more unruly and violent forms of contention by a group that is part of an opposition movement.[5] When radicalization slows down or reverses, it is often called *De-radicalization* (e.g., Bjørgo and Horgan 2009; Alimi et al. 2012, 2015; della Porta 2018). This Element is about the prevention of radicalization, namely, instances of contention wherein contending actors put a brake on the systematic, frequent adoption of violence – labeled here *Contained Radicalization* (Goodwin 2007; Alimi 2018; Brooke 2018; Malkki 2020; Busher et al. 2023). Specifically, it is about the history of relation-building within the settlement movement and between it and the Israeli state and its agents, which made it a story of contained radicalization despite the presence of factors identified in the literature as drivers of radicalization. Studying "exceptions to the rule" or negative cases is at least as important as learning "cases that prove the rule" (Emigh 1997; Burawoy 1998). As will be demonstrated, contained radicalization is not simply the absence of radicalization or its reversal, but a process in its own right.

1.2 The Puzzle

One dominant explanation for radicalization (and contained radicalization, for that matter) follows cognitive lines. Works in this cognitive tradition share the assumption that ideologies, worldviews, and other perceptual and cultural templates, such as identity, discourse, and consciousness, shape behavior, sometimes compellingly.[6] It follows then that a focus on values and ideologies held by movement actors suggests much about the development of a sense of inefficacy, counterculture, and, consequently, willingness to raise arms. Broadly speaking, then, when a given group holds an ideology or values that tolerate and justify the use of violence, we should expect the adoption of more unruly and violent forms of contention (e.g., Sprinzak 1998; Stern 2003; Asal and Rethemeyer 2008).

---

[5] Two clarifications. The omission of cognitive aspects from the definition is purposeful. It is possible to have group activists holding beliefs that increasingly justify intergroup violence (McCauley and Moskalenko 2008) without them engaging in actual violent behavior. While references to radical ideologies and goals constitute a central part of the analysis, they are seen as necessary yet insufficient drivers leading to engagement in violence. This is consistent with the Element's explanatory organizing principle according to which relations mediate the salience of such cognitive forces. To avoid further convolution, I use the terms *militants* and *militancy* when referring to instances where violence remains at the level of rhetoric (see della Porta 2013; Alimi et al. 2015).

[6] What I label here as cognitive, environmental, and relational lines of explanation is consistent with Tilly's (2003) classification of three camps in the study of collective violence. I prefer "cognitive" over Tilly's "idea people," and "environmental" over "behavioral people" to avoid confusion with this Element's focus on behavioral radicalization.

Works that follow cognitive lines to explain the radicalization of member groups of the settlement movement are in no short supply (Lustick 1988; Sprinzak 1991; Aran and Hassner 2013). Weisburd and Lernau's (2006) explanation for the lack of higher levels of violence during the anti-Pullout campaign is particularly noteworthy. The authors argue that the lack of settler violence related to what they call "normative balance." While many Jewish settlers held ideologies and values that justified violence, they "also voiced what can be defined as countervailing norms that discourage violence with other Israelis and encourage lawful behavior" (p. 43). Given the involvement of both Gaza Strip and West Bank settlers and the differences in their claims, ideology, and goals, as well as action strategy and tactics, the question remains of how such a normative balance was managed in actual situations and varying contexts relating, for example, to Palestinian attacks.

A second dominant explanation for radicalization follows environmental lines. Focusing on the autonomy of motives, impulses, and opportunities in the face of environmental stimuli as the origin of aggression, works following this tradition point to depletion of resources, greed, incentives for benefits, and an acute need for protection (e.g., Collier and Hoeffler 1999; Piazza 2006; Gupta 2008). From this point of view, when a group is exposed to environmental changes or events that undermine basic needs, such as security, or experiences profound perceptions of deprivation and anger, we should expect its members to engage in violence.

Among the settlement community, it would be difficult to exaggerate the shock, disbelief, and anger following the publication of the Gaza Pullout plan. This was particularly so in light of the continuing, at times intensifying, Palestinian attacks and rocket fire (inclusive of mortar shells – see Figure 2). Historically, instances of Jewish-settler violence against Palestinians increased whenever the former felt the Israeli political and security authorities provided them with insufficient protection or endorsed conciliatory measures and policies toward the latter (Weisburd 1989; Zertal and Eldar 2004; Pedahzur and Perliger 2009). During the Gaza Pullout campaign, a handful of violent attacks against Palestinians did take place close to and during the implementation of the plan, two of which resulted in the loss of Palestinian lives. It is telling, however, that the two lethal attacks were carried out when Palestinian rocket fire was no longer an issue, by individuals with no apparent organizational affiliations. Of greater significance is the fact that Palestinian attacks and rocket fire were a non-issue throughout the protest campaign in the sense of being unrelated to the level and form of contention of movement actors.

Figure 2 offers a graphic illustration of the puzzle. It plots weekly data on forms of contention by settlement movement member groups, incitements to

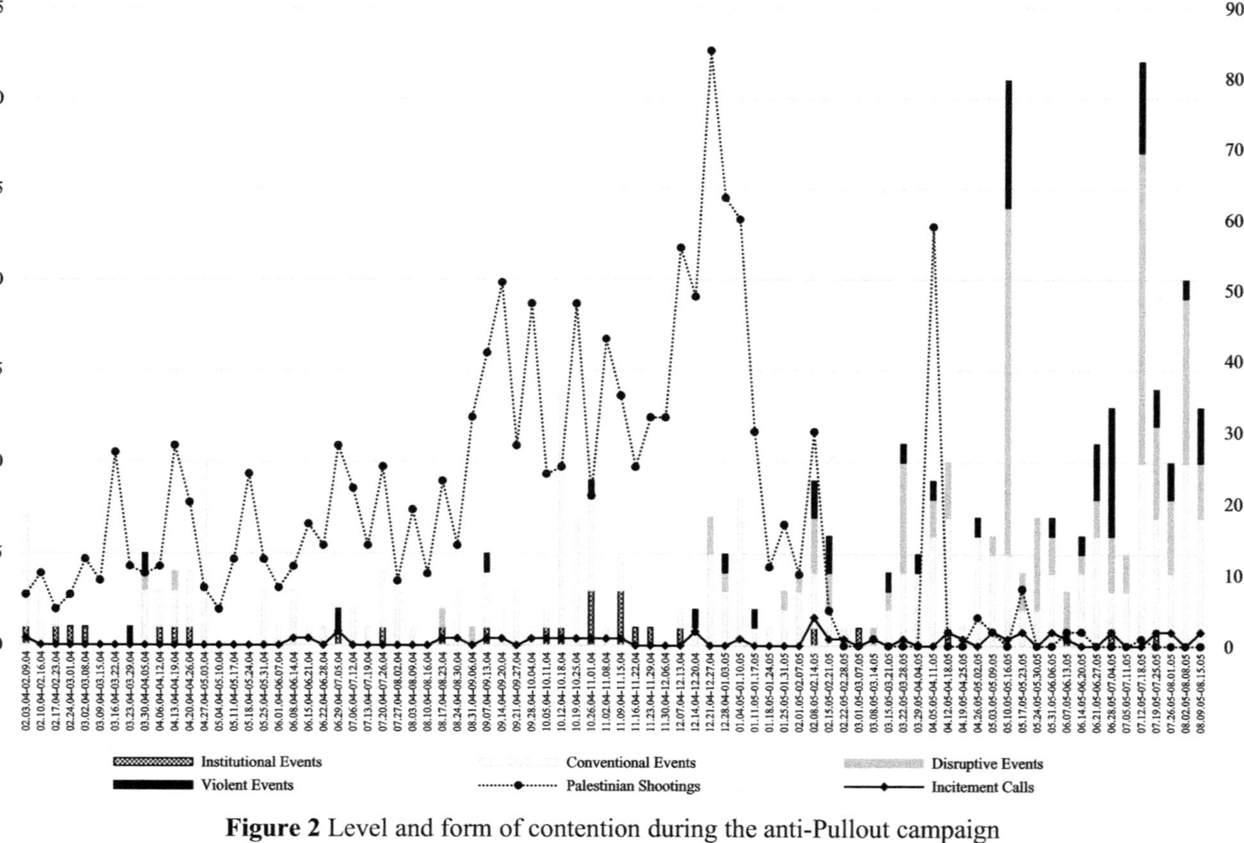

Figure 2 Level and form of contention during the anti-Pullout campaign

Source: Author's data.

Note: Unless stated otherwise, I obtained data on contention and response to contention from the coverage of the Israeli dailies *Yediot Achronot* and *Ha'Tzofe* and data on violence by these groups, and the number of Palestinian rockets and mortar firings during the entire campaign. Four points that stand out are the predominance of nonviolent forms of contention (i.e., events that do not involve property or bodily damage); the weak, inverse relation between movement actors' violence and Palestinian attacks ($r = -.24$), offering no support for the environmental line of explanation; the weak correlation ($r = .28$) between militancy and actual engagement in violence by movement activists, offering slim support for the cognitive line of explanation; and finally, the considerable portion of contentious activity clustered around specific events, for example, the Knesset's first reading of the "Disengagement Law" in late October 2004. The analysis of contained radicalization pays particular attention to these events, seen as representing critical shifts in patterns of contention and in media and public discourse (Staggenborg 1993; Alimi and Maney 2018).

1.3 The Solution: Relational Dynamics

The solution to the puzzle comes from relational sociology, particularly a strand called *relational realism*. Relational realism considers contacts, transactions, social ties, networks, and conversations as constituting the central stuff of social life, hence vital to understanding social and political phenomena (Emirbayer 1997; Tilly 2002, 2003; Diani 2003; Mische 2011). Relational sociologists contend that cognitive and environmental forces operate and gain (or lose) salience within social relations. Building on this reasoning, we can expect relational dynamics, for example, the ability of movement actors to mobilize consensus over strategy, tactics, and goals, to mitigate the influence of cognitive and environmental forces and, in turn, contain radicalization.

This Element builds on cumulative wisdom in relational realist-oriented research on radicalization processes to tell the story of contained radicalization in a potentially violent situation. This includes focusing on robust and recurring causal mechanisms to capture changes in relations as they unfold in arenas or fields of interaction between contending parties and actors within parties (e.g., the ability of two or more social movement groups to mobilize consensus over strategy, tactics, and goals). Recognizing that several forces usually constitute complicated processes like radicalization, relational realists pay analytical attention to the mutual influence of relational mechanisms as they combine to drive (or put a brake on) processes of radicalization (e.g., McAdam et al. 2001; Alimi et al. 2012, 2015; de Fazio 2013; della Porta 2013, 2018; Drevon 2022).[7]

---

[7] Instances of radicalization analyzed in this Element stop short at the stage of engagement in political violence by a social movement member organization. Processes of radicalization, however, may have additional stages, what has been labeled enhanced or post-radicalization (e.g., Alimi et al. 2015; Busher et al. 2023). At this enhanced stage, some mechanisms may

This Element adds to the growing body of work on the relational dynamics of radicalization by offering a historically sensitive analysis of how relations are built and evolve in their respective arenas. Because there is nothing inherent, determined, or linear to relation-building – even less so between contending parties – a historical analysis of this type helps to capture the temporal, contextual, contingent, reflective, and learned features of the process (Emirbayer and Mische 1998; Kurtz 2002). We will trace the process of the emergence and evolution of the constituent practices and routines of relational mechanisms and how they give rise to understandings, expectations, and rules of engagement.

Relatedly, this Element moves beyond the recognition that mechanisms and their respective arenas of operation mutually influence each other, and argues that such mutual influence is more dynamic and volatile than usually acknowledged. Mechanisms and their respective arenas of interaction are highly interdependent because, first, the class of events and occurrences that form a mechanism and unfold in one arena – practices and routines in the case of relational mechanisms – may have implications for other arenas. Mechanisms and arenas are highly interdependent also because actors may be involved and vested in more than one arena (Steinmo 2008; Alimi 2016). This Element offers a systematic examination and structured analysis of the mutual influence between mechanisms and the ways they co-evolve in variable ways, sometimes reinforcing and, at other times, undercutting each other. It brings together data on coordination to measure relational mechanisms, data on shared perception to measure cognitive mechanisms, and data on material conditions to measure environmental mechanisms. The combination of historical depth and methodological rigor allows for a nuanced examination of how relational mechanisms combine to mitigate the effects of cognitive and environmental mechanisms and, in turn, contain radicalization.

1.4 The Argument

Radicalization in the anti-Pullout campaign was contained as a result of the combined effect of three sets of relational dynamics that operated both between the main contending parties and within each one in ways that mitigated militancy and propensities for aggression and, in turn, promoted moderation. First, a brake on radicalization related to the ability of leaders from the central organizations of the movement to minimize competition and conflict over

---

operate differently and have different outcomes, namely, leading to (not away from) further radicalization. This is contingent on the stage of the conflict, the level of analysis (i.e., the "radical group" rather than the movement), and the composition of actors involved. An analysis along these lines of more recent instances of Jewish settler radicalization is offered in the Conclusion.

strategy, tactics, and goals among the various groups and organizations. The mechanism of *consensus mobilization*, referring to the formation and maintenance of legitimacy and convergence among movement organizations regarding action strategy, means, and goals (Klandermans 1988[8]; Diani 2000; McCammon 2003; Almeida 2007; Van Dyke and Amos 2017) captures these relational dynamics. Second, the ability to minimize competition and conflict was reinforced by clear and strictly kept rules of engagement between heads of the Israeli military and police and the movement leadership. These relational dynamics are captured by the mechanism of *underbidding*, which is about the willingness and ability of movement actors and agents of social control to establish and maintain understandings, expectations, and arrangements regarding the legitimate and acceptable scale, form, and scope of contention and repression (della Porta and Reiter 1998; Earl 2003; Gillham, Edwards, and Noakes 2013). Third, mutual reinforcement between consensus mobilization and underbidding broadened to include the ability of the movement leadership to generate meaningful input into the policymaking process throughout their campaign, based on a powerful strategic bargaining position. The mechanism of *opportunity spirals* captures the relational dynamics of changes in connections and ties that shape the interaction between movement actors and the political establishment. Following others, I define opportunity spirals as those actions, claims, and decisions by movement actors, elite allies, rivals, and authorities that strengthen a movement's strategic bargaining position from which it can generate political input (McAdam 1999; McAdam et al. 2001; Goldstone 2004).

The combined effect of these relational mechanisms mitigated the influence of extreme worldviews and environmental stimuli for aggression that movement activists held or experienced as forces pushing radicalization. Extreme worldviews emerged from the interaction between movement actors and the Israeli general public, including opposition forces, expressed in *polarization*, a cognitive mechanism defined as the increased ideological distance between movement actors (Alimi et al. 2015). Propensities for aggression emerged from the interaction between movement actors and actors of the Palestinian countermovement, expressed in *flanking*, an environmental mechanism defined as the disruption of daily routine and the undermining of basic needs (Alimi 2016). There was no shortage of movement actors holding fundamentalist religious worldviews that tolerated illegitimate and illegal behavior. Also present were movement actors who reacted to Palestinian attacks by initiating retaliatory

---

[8] Whereas Klandermans's (1988) original development of the concept centered on the micro-level (i.e., individual activists and participants), we analyze consensus mobilization in this Element at the group level.

attacks, often independently of, but sometimes against, Israeli security authority policy and instructions.

The mutual reinforcement of the three relational mechanisms and their combined moderating influence on militancy and propensities for aggression in the anti-Pullout campaign was the result of a long history of relation-building between the main contending parties. That history began to develop after the June 1967 War. It saw the emergence of relational practices and routines that constituted each of the three relational mechanisms and how they gradually configured the interactions between and within the main contending parties in specific ways. The first meaningful campaign against government policy prohibiting settlements in the upper West Bank region, known as the Sebastia campaign of 1974–1975, demonstrated this process of emergence most distinctly.

Changes in the set of opportunities and threats of a given contending party and other contingencies led to a divergence of interests and values between parties. These changes generated pressure on the evolution of one or more of the relational mechanisms. Often, the weakening or collapse of relational practices and routines that constituted one of the mechanisms undercut the others, in which case we saw an increase in the influence of extreme worldviews or aggressive propensities and, in turn, the progression of radicalization. The struggle against the Oslo Peace Process (1993–1995), which culminated in the tragic assassination of Prime Minister Rabin, is a case in point.

But there were also times, admittedly scarcer, when we saw reinforcing patterns developing between mechanisms. In this scenario, relational practices and routines of a given mechanism prevented further weakening of practices and routines that constituted another relational mechanism. The result was a lessening in the salience of those non-relational forces and, in turn, prevention of higher levels of violence. The campaign against the implementation of the peace treaty between Egypt and Israel (1978–1982), which culminated in the struggle against the evacuation of the Sinai Peninsula colonies, is a case in point.

Figure 3 offers a graphic summary of the main argument. As we will see, similar dynamics also occurred between campaigns, indicative of the features of reflective and learned relation-building. The fact that the dynamics of mutual reinforcement between the mechanisms and its moderating effect reached such a high degree of development in the anti-Pullout campaign should not lead us to assume it was inevitable. As subsequent sections demonstrate, the relation-building process and the eventual containment of radicalization in the Gaza Pullout was anything but deterministic or linear. It could have taken other paths at any given time, both before and during the anti-Pullout campaign, and, as indeed happened (and discussed in the Conclusion) during its aftermath.

Coordination**	Sebastia 1974-5*	Camp David 1978-82	First Intifada 1987-92	Oslo Accords 1993-5	Gaza Pullout 2004-5
High					Consensus Mobilization
					Underbidding
		Underbidding			Opportunity Spirals
Med					
		Opportunity Spirals		Consensus Mobilization	
			Underbidding		
Low	Consensus Mobilization		Opportunity Spirals		
	Underbidding			Underbidding	
	Opportunity Spirals		Consensus Mobilization		
Non		Consensus Mobilization			
				Opportunity Spirals	

Campaign

Figure 3 History of contentious interactions and relation-building

* Emergence of relational practices and routines

** Assessments of mechanisms along the coordination dimension pertain to campaigns in their entirety

1.5 Organization of the Element

This Element has three main sections. Each focuses on one relational mechanism, examining its emergence in the period surrounding the first campaign in Sebastia in 1974–1975, tracing its evolution during a specific past campaign, and analyzing how it exerted its moderating effects during the anti-Pullout campaign. Section 1 examines the emergence and evolution of consensus mobilization and how it configured the interactions between movement actors, paying particular attention to the campaign against the Camp David Accords; Section 2 examines the emergence and evolution of underbidding between movement actors and Israeli security forces, focusing on the struggle against the government's conciliatory policy in dealing with the First Palestinian Intifada; Section 3 follows suit and examines the emergence and evolution of the mechanism opportunity spirals between movement actors and the Israeli political establishment, and how it operated and exerted its effects on radicalization during the struggle against the Oslo Accords.

Theoretically, notwithstanding the focus on one relational mechanism in each section, attention is also paid to how the relational mechanism under investigation influences and is influenced by the other relational mechanisms. We will also pay attention to how relational dynamics mediate the respective salience of non-relational mechanisms and specify the possibility of radicalization. Historically, no matter how central specific past campaigns are claimed to be for the evolution of a given mechanism, additional meaningful developments that occur during other periods and campaigns are not overlooked. The goal of achieving a historically sensitive, longitudinal analysis is accomplished by making the coevolutionary analysis of the emergence and evolution of a particular mechanism integral to each section. The concluding section offers a discussion of three main takeaways for containing radicalization and how they help us make sense of recent instances of Jewish settler radicalization.

2 Intra-Movement Interaction and Consensus Mobilization

Social movements engaged in contentious collective action are "fields of actors," consisting of groups and organizations with differing positions and preferences regarding strategy, tactics, and goals. These differences typically reflect variations in interests, ideologies, and orientations toward the political establishment and other social categories. Even if a movement begins its campaign as reasonably homogenous, underlying differences will soon surface and can develop into competition and, possibly, conflict.

The Settlement Movement poses no exception in this regard. Despite the impressive breadth of consensus within the movement, there were thorny disagreements that often threatened to undermine the sheer ability to mobilize for action, sometimes deteriorating into intra-movement conflict. Indeed, there was nothing simple or plain-sailing about the process of relation-building among the various organizations and groups making up the movement. The ability to mobilize and maintain consensus over strategy, tactics, and goals met considerable challenges and witnessed significant failures. At times, relational dynamics unfolding in other arenas of interaction reinforced consensus mobilization. There were other times, however, when those relational dynamics undermined consensus mobilization. When this dynamic of coevolutionary relation-building became mutually reinforcing, it played a central role in mitigating the influence of violence-prone ideas and environmental stimuli for aggression. The result, as we will see, was contained radicalization.

2.1 The Emergence of Consensus Mobilization

Given the diversity of actors that became part of the consolidating settlement movement, how was consensus over goals, strategy, and tactics formed and, equally important, sustained? There were considerable disagreements between movement actors despite the convergence of interests and values between them, pertaining, for example, to the highest priority accorded to the land of Greater Israel and the importance of becoming an all-Israeli, cross-national movement. These disagreements related to (a) the primary goal of the movement and how to achieve it (i.e., a total transformation of society based on an uncompromising set of transcendental imperatives or a correction of society based on compromises and practical considerations), (b) the type of leadership and sources of authority (i.e., spiritual or field leadership or a combination of both), (c) the value and scope of Greater Israel (i.e., is the "promised land" a non-negotiable religious imperative, and what constitutes its exact territorial boundaries?), and (d) attitudes toward the Israeli-Jewish public (i.e., should the movement be attentive to the public or act as a revolutionary vanguard, and should the nonreligious Israeli-Jewish opposition be tolerated or be treated as traitors) (Lustick 1988; Sprinzak 1991).

Sources of tension became apparent, most notably following the February 1974 formation of the Bloc of the Faithful (Gush Emunim) as the movement's vanguard organization. They were expressed in disparate, sometimes conflicting strategies, tactics, and goals. For example, in late May 1974, in the wake of the October 1973 Yom Kippur War and pending a US-brokered disengagement agreement between Israel and Syria, a small group of settlers, organized as a settlement nucleus[9] called Elon Moreh, broke ranks. Members

---

[9] Typically, this is what all voluntary, pre-organized settlement groups were called, with the designated name of the would-be settlement appended. The case of the Elon Moreh nucleus was more complicated. It involved several contentious settlement bids that led to settlements with different names (e.g., Kedumim), before a settlement called Elon Moreh was approved in 1980.

refused the request of Golan Heights settlers to join in efforts to erect a settlement near the border between Israel and Syria. Despite calls by leaders of the Bloc in support of the Golan Heights settlement operation, Elon Moreh members preferred to focus on settling the upper West Bank region of Samaria – as indeed was the case in early June 1974 (see below) (Rubinstein 1982; Segal 1987).

The refusal of Elon Moreh members revealed not only disagreement regarding the value and scope of the Greater Land of Israel, but also the latent tension between religious and nonreligious elements in the movement. It is telling that when Bloc activists flocked to the Golan Heights in support, local activists who were members of the secular Kibbutz Marom Golan and behind the settlement initiative there were far from enthusiastic. Fully aware of the highly confrontational and anti-government character of the Elon Moreh settlement initiative in the West Bank, they feared their settlement "would turn into a Yeshiva with nobody left to work" (Rubinstein 1982: 55). According to Demant (1988), they yielded the enterprise to the Bloc only on the condition that they would accept relocation if the government ordered them to do so and refrain from violence. The insistence of Marom Golan settler activists on nonviolence expressed their concerns over the violent demonstrations organized by Hebron settlers and other right-wing activists against Secretary of State Kissinger's shuttle visits to Israel to conclude the disengagement agreement with Syria (Sprinzak Interview Collection, April 1986).

Despite these and other expressions of tension, there were attempts to mobilize consensus and, equally important, to sustain it. The lack of clear separation between field and spiritual leadership was perhaps the most central and consequential practice to emerge early on. On the one hand, some of the field leaders were also ordained rabbis, a position that granted them legitimacy and respectability vis-à-vis rank-and-file activists (Harnoy 1994). On the other, this spiritual leadership was present "on the ground," at times actively involved in resisting evictions. Thus, even if declaratively the most revered rabbis would unequivocally reject any compromise and join the others in fighting evictions, their actual presence and involvement, combined with their venerated stature, had a moderating effect. When security forces in early June 1974 came to evict Elon Moreh settlers from Hawara, a Palestinian village adjacent to Nablus, none other than Rabbi Kook, the spiritual father of the movement, was central in demonstrating passive resistance. He stubbornly clung to a barbed wire fence and refused to let go. Nevertheless, after a long day of resistance, he evacuated voluntarily and quietly, influencing the other squatters who followed suit (Segal 1987: 29–30; Huberman 2008: 79).

Furthermore, the fact that the two leadership cores were equally involved in ideological and practical matters and present in the Bloc's secretariat meetings facilitated decision-making and coordinating activities. A central decision reached early on by religious and secular leaders was not to let religious, *Halakhic* issues get in the way of settling the Greater Israel. According to Rubinstein (1982), the decision was made shortly after the Bloc and its secretariate, which included religious and secular representatives and set new standards of religious-secular cooperation, was formed. This decision, reflecting the importance Rabbi Kook attributed to the love and unity of the people of Israel, facilitated recruitment of secular supporters. Some of these recruits took an active role, at times the very initiative, in forming settlement nuclei and erecting new settlements. It was no coincidence that most settlements founded between 1968 and 1977 as a result of the movement's initiative had, at least initially, a mixture of religious and secular residents.

2.1.1 Early Challenges

Despite the best efforts on the part of the movement, attempts at consensus mobilization were only partially successful. Engagement in unruly and violent action continued to surface during the series of attempts (a total of seven "operations," as the movement called them) to settle in Samaria, specifically a desolate train station near the Palestinian village Sebastia. These operations took place between July 1974 and December 1975 and followed the attempt in Hawara by members of the Elon Moreh nucleus, discussed above.

Instances of settler violence were related to the still-fragile coordination and trust between the Bloc and the Elon Moreh nucleus. For example, during the third operation in early October 1974, despite a previous agreement to join hands, Elon Moreh activists acted independently of the Bloc and clashed with military forces (Demant 1988; *Yediot Achronot*, October 13, 1974). The fragility of consensus mobilization became even more evident during two subsequent operations in March 1975, initiated by members of the Elon Moreh nucleus. Nucleus members became frustrated by the continuing failure to generate sufficient political leverage and rejected the idea of doing so indirectly through public support, which would be gained, so it was hoped, by organizing mass processions to Sebastia. Instead, they decided to act independently of the rest of the movement organizations and clashed with military forces that came to evict them (Huberman 2008).

Other instances of violence had nothing to do with movement actors, nor with settlement drives. These instances amounted to brawls between pro-settlement and anti-settlement protesters during July and September 1974, resulting in light injuries and property damage (*Yediot Achronot*, July 26, 1974). They also included a handful of scattered attacks between Palestinian and Jewish residents in the city of Hebron during late 1974 and the summer of 1975. These attacks revolved mainly over praying arrangements at the sacred site of the Cave of the Patriarchs, as it is known to Jews, also called and known to Muslims as the Ibrahimi Mosque (Demant 1988; Sprinzak Interview Collection, April 1986).

However, examining the series of attempts to settle Sebastia and other contentious activity throughout the country suggests that instances of settler violence tended to decrease the more consensus mobilization was consolidated. Moreover, the patterns of interaction between the movement leadership and the government and between the movement and security forces reinforced the ability of movement leaders to sustain consensus mobilization. When the military or police were willing to negotiate with settler leaders and coordinate protests with policing, resistance and contention remained predominantly nonviolent. As further discussed in Section 2, this pattern began to emerge most notably and meaningfully during the second operation of late July 1974, when heads of the IDF negotiated a peaceful evacuation of Sebastia with settler leaders. As further discussed in Section 3, despite the reserved and unforthcoming approach of Prime Minister Rabin and some members of his government, movement leaders managed to foster an impressive network of support among politicians from an array of parties, even among Rabin's inner circle. The enhanced ability to exert meaningful pressure on the government facilitated consensus mobilization and was related to decreased militancy and violence.

2.1.2 Consensus Mobilization Faltered

Consensus mobilization faced ever-deepening challenges during the progression of the Camp David Accords between late 1977 and early 1979. However, it reached all-time low levels between March 1979 and April 1982 during the implementation of the Camp David Peace Accords (see Box 1). The gradual process of disintegrating coordination among movement actors resulted in higher levels of violence and instances of radicalization by both existing and newly formed organizations.

The movement leadership was already concerned with the inclusion of several "dovish" ministers in Prime Minister Begin's cabinet shortly after the Likud Party's victory in the May 1977 general elections, a success they took pride in making happen (discussed further in Section 3). Nevertheless, it would be fair to say that President Sadat's visit to Jerusalem in November 1977 caught the movement completely off-guard. It was the first time since June 1967 that the Israeli government was willing to retreat from a considerable part of the Occupied Territories – the Sinai Peninsula in this case – and evacuate around

	BOX 1 KEY DATES AND ACTORS: CAMP DAVID ACCORDS
May 17, 1977	Menachem Begin-led Likud's victory in the national elections
November 19	Egyptian President Sadat's visit to Israel
December 25	Begin and Sadat summit meeting in Egypt, followed by the Knesset approval of the peace plan three days later
March 7, 1978	The "officer Letter" marking the rise of Peace Now
September 18	Signing of the first Camp David Accord (approved by the Knesset on the 27th)
September 19	Heightened confrontation between Elon Moreh nucleus, IDF forces, and Minister of Defense in Rujeib results in a violent collision
October 12	Formation of the YESHA Council
March 26, 1979	Signing of the second Accord (peace treaty between Egypt and Israel), following the Knesset ratification on the 22nd
April 25	implementation of the peace treaty begins – withdrawal of IDF from the Sinai in several stages
October 9	Formation of the Tehiya (Revival) Party
October 22	Elon Moreh ruling
May 2, 1980	A killing of a Jewish settler in Hebron, leading to the first attack of the Jewish Underground (June 2)
May 5, 1981	Initial organizing of the Movement the Halt the Retreat in Sinai
August 5	Menachem Begin second term as Prime Minister
October 6	Assassination of President Sadat; establishment of illegal settlements by MHRS and *Kach*
February 27, 1982	Imposition of a military blockade on the Sinai
April 19–26	The struggle over Yammit – end of Israel's withdrawal

5,500 people from some twenty-two colonies and towns (Kliot and Albeck 1996). To make things worse, it soon became clear that the peace talks included the idea of Palestinian autonomy and a temporary freeze on new settlements.

Movement actors were not only alarmed by the recent developments, but also divided over how to respond. Some member organizations were willing to accept a certain measure of territorial compromise in exchange for peace with Israel's biggest enemy, while others, like Rabbi Kahane's *Kach* movement (see below), vehemently opposed the peace initiative (Sprinzak 1991). Additionally, while for some, it was not at all clear if the Sinai constituted an integral part of the "promised land" according to Jewish *Halakha*, others thought otherwise and were willing to act accordingly (Shafat 1995). Underlying this latter disagreement was also an ambivalent stance about the staunchly secular character of the Sinai colonies. Zertal and Eldar (2004) cite the words of a member of the Bloc, who published an apologetic article in the movement newsletter *Nekuda* (Hebrew for "point"), saying: "It is possible that the absence of 'settlements of our doing' in the Yammit region [i.e., Northern Sinai/Rafiah Salient] also contributed to this response of disregard" (p. 104; clarification added).

Disagreements over strategy and goals deepened and translated into defiant actions after it became clear that Prime Minister Begin and most of his cabinet members were not keen on moving forward with a large-scale settlement plan. Leaders of the movement presented the plan to Begin shortly before the elections and had received his enthusiastic support. When they found out they would only get six of the twelve settlements originally planned and that nuclei members would be placed in army camps, an intense debate broke out during the ensuing meeting of the Bloc secretariat. The eventual decision to accept the compromise, facilitated by Rabbi Kook's stance against anti-government settlement bids, was not followed by all of the nuclei. Indeed, two of them acted independently and were forcefully evicted by the military.

Later, defiant actions developed into blatant violence. On September 19, 1978, while Prime Minister Begin was still in Washington following the signing of the Camp David Accord, several members of the Elon Moreh nucleus broke ranks and initiated an illicit settlement bid near the village Rujeib, southeast of Nablus. The three days of struggle were unprecedented in terms of the resoluteness demonstrated and violence exercised not only on the side of the settlers but also on the part of the military forces and political authorities (e.g., settlers were besieged and deprived of water and food). It is telling that in Begin's absence, both the acting prime minister and the minister of defense refused to follow the open-door routine that had developed between leaders of the movement and the prime minister. As discussed in subsequent sections, the Minister of Defense offhandedly dismissed a compromise the Chief of General Staff eventually tried to work out.

Fully aware of the potentially devastating and counterproductive anti-government settlement bids, several grassroots activists took the initiative and formed the YESHA Council (heretofore, the Council; a Hebrew acronym for Judea, Samaria, and Gaza) in October 1978. Its declared aims were to coordinate efforts between the growing number of settlements, to thwart the Palestinian autonomy plan, and to sustain the settlement enterprise they believed the government had abandoned (Roth 2005). Alas, these efforts did little to alleviate the tensions and disagreements and restore consensus; in fact, the formation of the Council reflected and reinforced existing ones. Because it was essentially semi-institutional, comprising heads of local and regional councils and partly funded by the state, it was seen by many as a body not truly willing to engage in a struggle against the institution it depended on. Equally important was the omission of the Sinai Peninsula from the acronym of the Council, which became symbolic of the greater weight given to *Halakhic* issues among movement actors. More broadly, this omission indicated the growing salience of polarization emerging between the movement and Israeli progressive left-wing forces, projecting its effects on relations between religious and secular elements within the movement. It soon became clear that the dominant voices within the movement treated the struggle against the Sinai pullout as secondary, and that many of those who went to the Sinai to protest evacuation were essentially struggling for Hebron in the West Bank (Segal 1999).

Despite occasional tensions between secular and religious activists, and notwithstanding the emergence of organized progressive opposition forces, polarization operated in low gear with little effect on radicalization. The most influential of these progressive opposition forces emerged in March 1978: Peace Now (*Shalom Achshav*). The movement took shape following a letter drafted by a group of several hundred reserve officers and sent to Prime Minister Begin with a blunt warning that only a peace-seeking Israel that exhausted all possible means for attaining peace would continue to enjoy the support of its soldier-citizens (Kaminer 1996). Shortly after, the movement began to call for immediate withdrawal from the Occupied Territories and organized peace rallies throughout the country, which gained increasing traction and popularity. Nevertheless, when members of Peace Now went to a new settlement site north of Ramallah in early August 1978 to protest against its pending approval, settler activists refrained from any act of counter-protest and even offered them food (Rubinstein 1982). This response was not necessarily an indication of contempt on the part of the movement activists but rather one of confidence in the political efficacy of the movement coupled with the dominance of the *Mamlakhti* approach and the value of "settling in the hearts" of Israeli Jews (Feige 2009).

2.2 Collapsed Consensus Mobilization and Radicalization

The violent eviction of the Elon Moreh and Bloc activists from Rujeib became a prelude to an unprecedented escalation of violence and the first meaningful expressions of radicalization in the West Bank and Northern Sinai. During that violent eviction, some activists refused to follow a call for restraint by Rabbi Kook from his sickbed[10] and later, during a Bloc secretariate meeting, openly questioned that call. Some of these activists went so far as to withdraw from the movement, began to adopt mystical-Kabalistic worldviews, and went underground. Following additional obstacles to settling Elon Moreh, more activists adopted a confrontational approach. They opposed all compromises, including those the movement as a whole supported.

On December 26, 1979, several leading Bloc figures and activists joined Rabbi Kahane and his *Kach* followers in disrupting a visit of Prime Minister Begin to Hebron (*Davar*, December 27, 1979, p. 4). From only one prior record of contact between Kahane and Bloc activists from Hebron in August 1976,[11] a growing number of movement activists were now willing to accept an organization the secretariat had theretofore rebuffed. Despite several attempts as early as 1974 by Kahane to reach out and become acceptable to the movement, he had been utterly rejected, seen as a cultural outsider (having immigrated to Israel from the US in 1971), and repudiated for his preferred strategy of violence and terrorism (Sprinzak 1991; Shafat 1995). This type of "convergence at the margins" broadened to include militants from the Sinai colonies. It was consolidated further by the active support of notable veteran Bloc leaders such as Rabbi Levinger, who had already withdrawn from the movement and gone underground. Members of this newly formed grouping presented an intense, trenchant opposition to the YESHA Council and other more pragmatic Bloc leaders on almost all issues.

In the context of collapsed coordination among the various movement organizations, polarization gained momentum and began souring relations between religious and secular activists. Although the widening ideological distance remained at the rhetorical level, it was nonetheless meaningful. One telling example occurred in late 1980 when several Bloc leaders pressured the Council to stop providing municipal services to the West Bank settlement Salyit because it was predominantly secular (Harnoy 1994).

But while it remained mainly rhetorical, flanking was not. Palestinian attacks on Jewish settlers throughout the Territories were more consequential, pushing forward a shift in the targets of settler violence. What began as a quiet withdrawal of two activists from the movement in 1978 developed into a network of like-minded activists for whom the central problem of the people of Israel was how to resume the process of redemption that was brought to a halt at Camp

---

[10] At the time, Rabbi Kook was too sick to be actively involved in settlement bids and passed away in March 1982, a month before the evacuation of Yammit.

[11] Following indications that the Rabin government was about to renege on the Sebastia compromise (discussed in Section Three).

David. The means to that end was the removal of the "abomination" – the Dome of the Rock on the Temple Mount (Al-Aqsa) – to undermine the Camp David Accords and, in the process, bring about a new dynamic of redemption (Sprinzak 1991; Pedahzur and Perliger 2009; Aran and Hassner 2013). The network of nearly thirty coconspirators from settlements throughout the country – later known as the Jewish Underground – did not realize their grand plan. However, before the exposure and arrest of its members in April 1984, it did carry out a series of lethal terrorist attacks against Palestinians, launched in response to the killing of a yeshiva student in Hebron. These attacks included, for example, severely injuring several Palestinian mayors by blowing up their cars and a shooting attack at the Muslim College of Hebron,[12] resulting in the death of three students and the injury of thirty-three.

But while the Underground conducted its activities in secrecy, some of its members were also involved in the struggle against evacuating the Sinai colonies and towns. This struggle became particularly ferocious during the destruction of Yammit, located in the northern Sinai. There, they joined forces and cooperated with Kahane's *Kach* activists and a newly formed organization that became central in leading the struggle: the Movement to Halt the Retreat in Sinai (MHRS). Several Bloc veterans, Elon Moreh members, and representatives from other settlements (including two from the Sinai) resented the relative neglect and lack of more meaningful involvement in the struggle against the implementation of the peace treaty on the part of the Bloc as a whole, in particular the Council.

Following initial meetings in May 1981, these activists launched the first public activities of MHRS in October of that year (Aran 1985). While many of MHRS's contentious activities were conventional, its mode of action was predominantly disruptive and violent, such as initiating organized infiltrations following the sealing of the region (Wolfsfeld 1988; Sprinzak 1991). The struggle shifted to higher gears of intensity and lethality following the imposition of a blockade on the Sinai region on February 27, 1982. The blockade followed a dramatic increase in inflammatory rhetoric and incitement, which frequently and forcefully translated into violence. The rise in militancy indicated a weakening of the movement's bargaining position, and was accompanied by slandering rhetoric in retaliation on the part of Prime Minister Begin and his close circle. What started as antagonizing rhetoric and accusations by Begin and his camp that movement actors were messianic and enemies of peace broadened to include attacks on the IDF for being too soft on activists. It reached

---

[12] Later named Hebron University.

critical levels during the last weeks of the struggle when Prime Minister Begin and his staff refused to talk to leaders of MHRS (Segal 1999: 127, 190).

On the one side, settler activists engaged in uncompromising violent confrontations with the police and military forces, refusing to follow a call for restraint by Israel's chief rabbis (Segal 1999). Many settler activists engaged in the destruction of security force property and had actual fistfights with soldiers and police officers, slapping their faces and throwing stones and Molotov cocktails at them. Hundreds of others entrenched themselves on rooftops and actively resisted eviction, and a group of *Kach* activists fortified themselves in a public shelter with explosives, ammunition, and cyanide capsules, threatening to kill themselves if forced to leave.[13] But violence was not only the doing of ultra-radical movement activists. Although overreaction and brutality were mostly evident among the police and border guard units, military forces too played a role in the cycle of violence. There were instances of soldiers engaging in intense, humiliating beatings; extensive use of water and foam cannons; and the use of axes to smash windows and doors, all taking place while bulldozers destroyed the town.

Importantly, however, IDF senior officers began to make efforts to calm the situation and maintain contact and a dialogue with the resisters as part of an overall approach of restraint and containment. This approach of the IDF, which broadened to include joint efforts with several Knesset members and chief rabbis to reestablish communication and restore contact between movement actors and the government, proved crucial in preventing higher and more lethal levels of violence. We return to the moderating effects of the IDF approach in Section 2.

The post-Yammit period saw a pattern of continuing disintegration of consensus mobilization. Attempts to patch things up and reestablish consensus shortly after the destruction of the town, later during the height of the first Palestinian Intifada (1987–1992 – discussed in Section 2), and still later during the Rabin-led government's peace initiatives (1993–1995 – discussed in Section 3), were partly successful at best. The realization of the need to close ranks in the face of what was seen as the most severe test of the robustness of the settlement enterprise (i.e., the first Intifada) and then of the enterprise's sheer integrity, if not existence (i.e., the Oslo Accords) acted as a necessary yet insufficient factor for mobilizing consensus. Even when this realization proved somewhat successful and prompted a certain degree of convergence at the movement level, it lacked reinforcing patterns of interactions between the

---

[13] As part of efforts to mend the relationship between the movement and the government, Prime Minister Begin agreed to personally ask Rabbi Kahane for help in convincing his followers to surrender, as indeed happened.

movement and the Israeli political establishment (i.e., opportunity spirals) and between the movement and the Israeli security forces (i.e., underbidding). As we have seen and will continue to see in subsequent sections, the absence of mutually reinforcing relational dynamics facilitated the increase in the salience of flanking and polarization and, in turn, pushed forward instances of settler radicalization. At this stage, we can learn about the eventual development of such patterns of mutual reinforcement by analyzing how consensus mobilization was successfully created and maintained during the most formidable challenge the movement had ever faced.

2.3 Consensus Mobilization in the Gaza Pullout

The anti-Pullout campaign was no exception in terms of the need to cope with the sources of tension between and among the multiple organizations of the movement. However, the unprecedented gravity and scope of the disengagement plan made intra-movement interactions a highly volatile arena and the importance of managing consensus exceptionally acute. The acuteness of such a task stemmed from the cumulative history of several struggles, some of which produced hostility, mutual distrust, and newly formed organizations.

Table 1 classifies most organizational actors involved in the anti-Pullout campaign according to their primary strategy and tactics, ideological outlook regarding state and society, targets, and goals. As if these differences were not enough, additional ones made consensus mobilization even more challenging. These differences related most centrally to resources and legitimacy among the settler population, with the Council holding the upper hand, and to the antici-pated cost and sacrifice entailed in the implementation of the pullout, concern-ing which the *Va'ad Ha'Peula Gush Katif* (Gush Katif Action Committee; heretofore GKAC) was undoubtedly primary. According to a spokesperson for the radical student organization the Orange Cell when asked about internal relationships within the movement, "[T]here were countless tensions among the various worldviews, those who primed the struggle over the hearts and minds of the public and those who promoted the idea of struggle over the Land of Israel ... those who sought to disengage and those who wanted to engage." Nevertheless, despite the unprecedented diversity of groups and organizations involved in the campaign, perhaps its most noticeable feature was the sustained consensus over nonviolent action strategy and the goal of abolishing the Plan.

Following publication of the Disengagement Plan in early February 2004, it became clear to and accepted by all movement actors that the Council and GKAC would lead the campaign. The two also agreed early on that the final word on strategic and tactical issues should lie with GKAC. Without underestimating the

Table 1 Typology of movement organizations in the anti-Pullout campaign

Organization	Strategy & Tactics	Ideological Outlook	Target & Arena	Goals
Gush Katif Action Committee**	Persuasion and engagement; conventional (e.g., processions, vigils)	Moderate, integrationist	Public	Abolish the Plan
YESHA Council; The Legal Forum**; Women in Green	Cooperation and Bargaining; Institutional and conventional (e.g., Lobbying, Litigation, demonstrations)	Pragmatic, integrationist	Political Authorities; Public; Media;	Prevention of territorial withdrawals and settling the OT
Orange Cell**; The National House**; YESHA Rabbis Committee;	Confrontational and Resistance; Disruptive (e.g., street blocking; insubordination)	Radical, conditional integrationist	Designated publics (e.g., students); Jewish Diaspora; YESHA Council	Opposition to the Plan, integrity of the Land of Israel, and Halakhic way of life
National Jewish Front; Gamla Shall Not Fall Again; Jewish Heart; *Kach*/Kahane Chai; Hilltop Youth	Intimidation and Coercion; Violence	Extremist, segregationist	Palestinians, Progressive organizations, YESHA Council, security forces	Redefining the Movement; transforming state and society

** Stands for newly formed organizations

value of the four northern Samaria settlements, it was beyond doubt that Gush Katif settlers were the ones who would bear the brunt of the pullout. Even when the Council preferred acting politically through intense lobbying, trusting it was the most promising and effective venue, it nonetheless "toed the line" with GKAC's *Mamlakhti*-like integrationist approach and preferences regarding the direct educational and information campaign it carried out vis-à-vis the public. The Council also made sure to support GKAC financially and operationally. A leading figure in the Council provided insight into the sources of coordination within the movement:

> There were representatives participating in each side's working meetings … while there were disagreements, they tended to be tactical … of course, we were influential given the resources we had, but we could not dictate things as they [GKAC] were the ones who were about to pay the highest price if we failed, so we toed the line even when we thought they were too passive and restrained.

The more evidence of success the GKAC provided, the easier it became for the Council to continue supporting its preferred action strategy and goals, and the easier it became for both to secure the cooperation of the ultra-radical and extremist organizations. For example, all movement actors agreed that credit for inducing Prime Minister Sharon to agree to bring the pullout plan to a vote by members of the Likud Party Central Committee in May 2004 and for their victory should go to GKAC. Their success in convincing two-thirds of Likud members to vote against the plan resulted from the weeks-long public campaign organized by the GKAC. The operation, named "face-to-face," involved visiting the homes of tens of thousands of registered Likud members throughout the country and talking them out of supporting the plan.

The fact that Prime Minister Sharon eventually went against his promise to respect the results of the internal referendum did little to detract from GKAC's newly established standing, which continued to consolidate following subsequent successful nationwide representations of support and commitments. Nonetheless, Sharon's success in having a "modified" plan approved by the government in June 2004 led to a surfacing of dissenting voices on the part of ultra-radical and extremist organizations.

Calls for violence began to appear following government approval of the pullout plan in early June 2004. These calls, however, became more frequent, severe, and concrete surrounding the preliminary Knesset reading for approval of the plan in late October 2004. These expressions of militancy included publicized analogies between Sharon and Hitler and, alarmingly, carrying out a *pulsa dinura*[14] ceremony

---

[14] Aramaic for lashes of fire. A Kabbalistic ceremony in which the biblical angels of destruction are conjured up to prevent forgiveness of a person's sins and curse them to death.

on him. As will be further discussed in Section 2, this was also when Palestinian Kassam rocket and mortar fire from Gaza Strip was at its height, with 156 missiles fired by Palestinian activists during the month following Knesset approval.

Nevertheless, radicalization of rhetoric and militancy did not translate into behavioral radicalization. For a central leader of the Council, it was about "staying relevant, as turning to violence is like breaking the rules of the game, and once we do that, we could no longer be part that game." This emphasis on *Mamlakhtiyut* and the importance of remaining connected to the general public was also voiced by one of the leaders of GKAC, stating that "violence would only have distanced us and disconnect us from the Israeli public." Relating to the issue of Palestinian rocket fire, the interviewee made a revealing link between relational and environmental dynamics, saying, "We kind of hoped it would act to our benefit . . . even the heads of the army thought the plan made no sense. The deteriorating security situation brought about many newcomers, many more than people who decided to leave. If at all, the increase in rocket fire had the opposite effect."

Figure 4 presents corroborating findings from a content analysis of coverage by several movement-based newspapers (representing the central "voices" within the movement and the Religious-Zionist public more broadly) following five critical events. When the overall valence of a given item conveyed

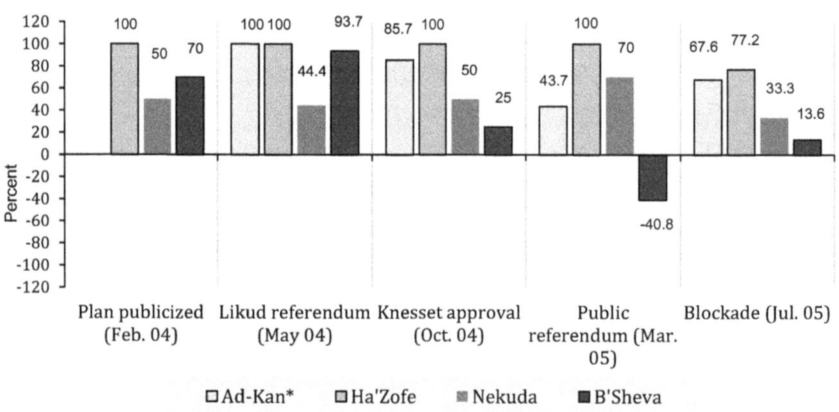

Figure 4 Integrationist talk by newspaper and events

* First appearance in early February containing opening statements and Gush Katif community-related information

Source: Alimi, Eitan Y. 2018. "Struggling to Remain Relevant": Why and How Radicali-zation Was Impeded in the Struggle against the Gaza Pullout." *Canadian Review of Sociology*, 55(4): 597–623.

Mamlakhtiyut, it was coded as "integrationist talk" and when a media item stressed anti-*Mamlakhtiyut*, it was coded as "segregationist talk." Coverage containing references to both *Mamlakhtiyut* and anti-*Mamlakhtiyut* was coded as *mixed*. A score for each period was calculated based on the coded items of each media outlet.[15]

The main point worth noting is how nuanced and dynamic an "integrationist talk" score is, responsive to political contexts and ideological outlooks. The coverage of *Ha'Zofe*, representing the moderate stance of the Religious-Zionist population, maintains, as expected, a steadily high integrationist score. Yet, the imposition of the blockade over the Gaza Strip was associated with a relative drop in that score. The coverage of *Ad-Kan*, the weekly newsletter of the ideologically moderate GKAC, is also high on *Mamlakhtiyut*, yet presents more significant variations, which is expected given the unique position of the Gaza Strip settlement population. Compared to the considerably lower, albeit consistently integrationist score of *Nekuda*, the voice of the more pragmatic Council, variations in *B'Sheva's* coverage, representing the radical and extremist organizations, are particularly telling. Following the failure to pass the Public Referendum Act, an event that marked the onset of a full-fledged direct-action campaign, there is a clear drop in *B'Sheva's* "integrationist talk" score. Yet, during that month, only a few violent actions were reported. This finding is particularly revealing given that the start of the direct-action campaign also saw increased protest activity by pro-pullout groups and organizations, such as the *Ha'Mifkad Ha'Leumi* (Hebrew for National Census). In contrast, following the imposition of the blockade, when settler violence began to accrue, *B'Sheva's* coverage reflected higher levels of integrationist talk.

Revealingly, one of the most extremist activists in the campaign, a former *Kach* member, and, at the time, leader of the ultra-radical organization Jewish National Front, offered insights that help make sense of the findings. Speaking from the hindsight of the post-Pullout internal rebellion against the Council and the surge of settler violence (on which we will say more in the concluding section) and making sure not to let his resentment of the Council and GKAC go unnoticed, he stated:

> All they [GKAC and YESHA] cared about was to win the hearts and minds of the public ... we failed to win that struggle because they refused to go all the way. They are the ones to be blamed. What they wanted was to influence the public and the politicians. I couldn't do much about that ... you cannot win with this kind of people and approach, so I was forced to play along.

---

[15] The score is based on the sum of the "integrationist talk" positive percentage, plus half of the "mixed" percentage, minus the "segregationist talk" negative percentage.

Awareness of the dangerous potential of the ultra-radical organizations, in particular their inflated militancy, prompted the Council and GKAC to deepen and broaden their coordination efforts. What "forced" the Jewish National Front leader and other leaders and activists of ultra-radical organizations to play along had something to do with three related relational routines and practices that reflected lessons learned by some members of the more veteran leadership based on their experience from past struggles like Yammit and the Oslo Accords.

In addition to establishing and maintaining channels and forums for exchange of information, the Council and GKAC acted preemptively to diffuse the potential for violence. The more profound the disillusionment among activists regarding the chances of preventing the pullout through institutional channels and lawful behavior became, particularly after the failure to pass the Public Referendum Act of late March 2005, the more proactive the Council and GKAC became. First, the joint GKAC and YESHA leadership made sure to harness the support of the central rabbis of the Religious-Zionist public sector, in particular those in the settler community. They obtained their approval for each decision and at times asked them to be physically present at protest events. A telling case was the mass rally called the "connection march" (discussed at the beginning of the introduction to this Element) that was meant to break into Gush Katif immediately following the imposition of the Gaza blockade in mid-July 2005. The spiritual leadership's backing and involvement included those moderate and pragmatic rabbis for whom *Mamlakhtiyut* was a guiding principle. Given the participation of the most prestigious and revered rabbis of the time, even the more extremist rabbis and, by extension, their followers, hesitated to break ranks.

Harnessing the support of the rabbis and securing their participation in turn helped the moderate and pragmatic leadership to maintain its hold over the campaign. It empowered its past credentials of successfully managing challenges and struggles with religious affirmation and backing. Thus, even when certain rabbis nevertheless stated it was religiously permissible for individual religious soldiers to refuse to participate in the pullout, it was clear to the entire Religious-Zionist public and settlement population that the most revered rabbis supported the leadership. Indeed, lack of such support and backing would have been seen as a sweeping call for insubordination, which could have meant an outright rebellion against the IDF and the state. As discussed in Section 3, this was precisely the type of sweeping rabbinical ruling permitting insubordination that pushed Prime Minister Rabin and the leaders of the movement further apart and facilitated radicalization during the struggle against the Oslo Accords.

This empowerment, however, could not have sufficed in and of itself. It required continuing efforts by the Council and GKAC to demonstrate their competence and credibility and to cement their legitimacy vis-à-vis their public, a practice similar to what Einwohner (2007) calls "authority work." These efforts involved intensive parliamentary and legal activity; countless vigils, marches, demonstrations, and public prayers; along with more disruptive activities including road blocks, and interfering with public ceremonies. As discussed in the following sections, substantial backing from local military officers and powerful political leverage contributed to these efforts.

Last but certainly not least, the leadership realized that a helpful way to contain ultra-radical elements would be to secure their collaboration. In addition to admitting that they fully knew that they "must not blink or hesitate before them [i.e., ultra-radical leaders and activists]," a leader of the Council also revealed that he and other leading figures in the Council "constantly talked to them, as their feedback was important ... I admit that Marzel [a leader of the Jewish National Front] is a better tactician than me. Besides, had we pushed them aside, they would have dissociated themselves from us."

In this regard, a telling illustration is that immediately following the failure to pass the Public Referendum Act in late March 2005, the Council initiated the formation of the Joint Headquarters, a forum that comprised most of the organizations (including the ultra-radical ones). Thus, it was not too infrequent that the leadership purposely contacted ultra-radical leaders to ask for their advice and assistance. Within this framework, for example, none other than the leader of the Jewish National Front was in charge of dissuading the ultra-orthodox political party *Shas* from joining Sharon's coalition as part of the systematic (and successful in this case) effort to narrow the government's base of parliamentary support.

The social-network analysis data in Figure 5 captures some of these relational dynamics and additional ones with other actors and parties, which combined to bolster consensus mobilization surrounding the Gaza Pullout. When observing the contacts mapped among various key actors[16] during the month following the failure to pass the Public Referendum Act (March 29, 2005–April 29, 2005), the first thing to note is the relatively high density of the network. The high number of contacts between each pair of actors (e.g., thirteen contacts between GKAC and Knesset actors) and the small number of *indirect* contacts for each actor illustrate this. The only exception is with the ultra-radical organizations, which, while exhibiting the smallest number of three *direct* contacts, were the most meaningful ones for mobilizing consensus and, consequently, containing radicalization.

---

[16] LEGAL stands for the legal system; KATIF for GKAC; PM for Prime Minister and related bodies; PUBOFF for Public officials/figures; RADIC for radical and extremist organizations; PAR for Knesset; GOVERN for government; and RABBI for rabbis.

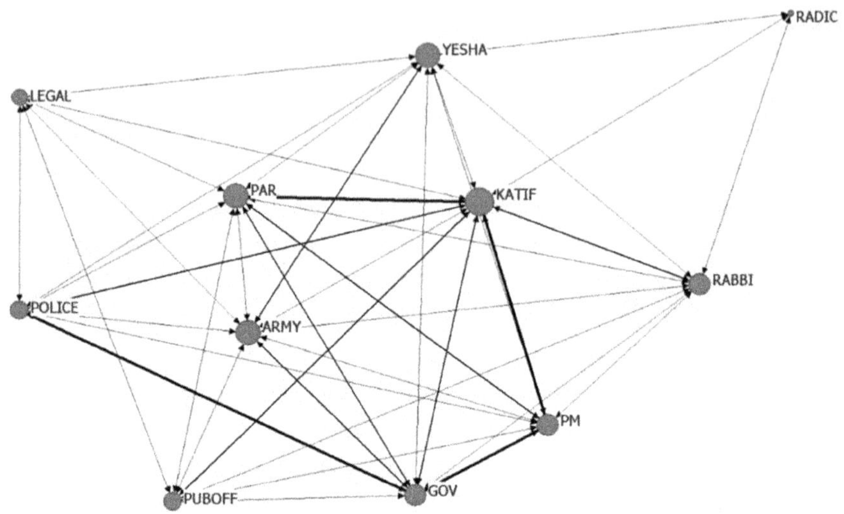

Figure 5 Network of ties among Gaza Pullout actors

Source: Alimi, Eitan Y. 2018. "Struggling to Remain Relevant": Why and How Radicalization Was Impeded in the Struggle against the Gaza Pullout." *Canadian Review of Sociology*, 55(4): 597–623.

3 Movement–Army Interaction and Underbidding

The patterns of interaction between movement actors and agents of social control constitute another equally important framework of relational dynamics for understanding the process of contained radicalization. Rather than treating the repression – contention nexus as unfolding between two independent players, scholars have argued for the importance of analyzing how agents of social control and movement actors engage in learning processes and constantly adapt in their interactions. Agents of social control – the military, the police, and other security forces and agencies – are the ones who engage with activists "on the ground" and make decisions that, at times, are beyond what is required by law or at odds with formal political directives and are occasionally ambiguous. Underbidding is about how agents of social control and movement leaders negotiate and manage understandings and agreements regarding the legitimate and acceptable styles of protest and policing.

As in Section 1, we first analyze the emergence of underbidding between the movement and Israeli agents of social control during the Sebastia campaign of 1974–1975. We will also show how, despite the meaningful convergence of interests and values between Israeli agents of social control and the movement that emerged following the June 1967 War, the process of relation-building was highly contingent, fleeting, and reversible. The analysis of the evolution of the mechanism of underbidding, however, focuses in particular on the first Palestinian Intifada, before returning to how it played out during the anti-Pullout campaign.

3.1 Conducive Conditions for Underbidding

The unprecedented Israeli victory in the June 1967 War and the taking over of territories that more than tripled its size gave rise to meaningful changes in the convergence of values and interests between the IDF and activists and leaders of the would-be Settlement Movement. Before June 1967, that convergence prompted the development of a unique accommodative framework called *Yeshivot Hesder* (lit. arrangement yeshivas) that enabled Religious-Zionist youth to combine advanced Torah studies with combatant military service. Following the War, the scope and depth of convergence went through considerable changes. Many members of the Religious-Zionist public saw the swift and glorious military victory as a "miraculous divine act." It liberated those territories considered part of the Promised Land and signified the beginning of the redemption of the Jewish People. While traditionally considered an elevated duty within the Religious-Zionist public, conscription to the IDF became a holy calling, and the IDF acquired a sacred status (Cohen 1993). The fact that the IDF became the sovereign power in the Territories following 1967[17] added an essential practical dimension to this "holy calling" from the vantage point of growing numbers of Religious-Zionist youths and, increasingly, members of the settlement community.

For the IDF, enlisting Religious-Zionist youth and facilitating their integration within the military framework took on added value following the expansion of Israel's borders and increased security tasks. Indeed, it was not just the need for quality military forces, but also the realization on the part of the IDF (and the Israeli government) that controlling the vast Territories necessitated involvement of the Jewish population there in daily security tasks. This realization became concrete following the October 1973 Yom Kippur War, which saw the immediate crumbling of the military-post-based lines of defense along the borders with Egypt and Syria and prompted a renewed interest in the Area Defense System (ADS). The ADS was to be based on settlements and manned by their residents, who would be armed and trained; it become part of the overall defense system designed to complement the IDF's tasks (Kimmerling 1979).

---

[17] Except for East Jerusalem, where Israeli law was already implemented in 1968 (unilaterally annexed in 1980), and the Golan Heights (unilaterally annexed in 1981).

Even with the enhanced convergence of interests and values between the IDF and movement actors, ample sources of tension made the emergence of underbidding challenging. For example, as the sovereign power in the Territories, the IDF maintained law and order and safeguarded the rights of all its populations. This meant, among other things, that the IDF conducted arrests of both Jewish and non-Jewish lawbreakers,[18] which naturally became a constant source of tension with the settlers. There was also no shortage of sources of tension stemming from the movement. The fact that the settlement population became embedded within the Israeli defense system meant that settler leaders kept pushing to be more actively involved in tactical matters and, crucially, in shaping IDF policy. Still, leaders of the movement and senior IDF officers managed to build relations based on practices and routines that ultimately gave rise to understandings, expectations, and arrangements regarding the legitimate and acceptable scale, form, and scope of contention and repression.

3.2 The Emergence of Underbidding

During the first stages of the Sebastia campaign of 1974–1975, when consensus mobilization was still fragile, settlers' form of contention remained predominantly nonviolent and organizationally coordinated whenever senior IDF officers adopted an approach of negotiated management. Indeed, the Sebastia campaign became the first meaningful "trial by fire" for both sides. Each side learned from one settlement operation to the next and adjusted its approach to that of the other, while being responsive to the approaches of additional actors.

Following the launch of the second Sebastian operation in late July 1974, Chief of General Staff Mordechai Gur expressed his disapproval of the Government's directive to evict the settlers by force. CGS Gur warned the government that "this is a very serious movement . . . not a simple insubordinate group . . . you do not use the army against such a major social and political movement" (Zertal and Eldar 2004: 386; see also Shafat 1995). What was telling about the stance of the CGS was his subsequent actions, which made clear what he had meant by "a very serious movement." Instead of letting local officers or even the commander of the Central Command[19] handle the eviction,

---

[18] Police forces were subordinated to the IDF and were responsible for investigating Jewish law breakers vis-à-vis the state attorney, which expectedly strained relations with the settlement population. The hierarchy between the IDF and the police made the interaction between the former and the movement much more meaningful and central. References to the police and other security forces will be made in so far as they serve the overall argument.

[19] Security-wise, Israel is divided into three regional commands: Northern, which includes the Golan Heights; Central, which includes the West Bank and East Jerusalem; and Southern, which includes the Gaza Strip and, until 1982, the Sinai Peninsula.

as was usually the case, CGS Gur decided to arrive on the scene. Upon arrival, exercising his discretion, he approached the movement leadership to try to talk them into voluntary and peaceful evacuation and to agree on acceptable modes of resistance. After a lengthy meeting, during which it was decided on voluntary evacuation and passive resistance only, Gur informed the crowd of hundreds of activists about the agreement and announced that he ordered soldiers to refrain from using force. Moreover, Gur remained on-site to oversee the evacuation. While not all activists voluntarily evacuated, they did not resist when carried out by soldiers (*Ha'aretz*, July 30, 1974; *Yediot Achronot*, July 29, 1974; Zertal and Eldar 2004; Peri 2006; Huberman 2008).

Subsequent operations and evictions from Sebastia did not necessarily involve the CGS. Still, they did involve the chief of the Central Command, who consistently tried to engage in unmediated consultation with heads of the movement (Demant 1988). These practices of respecting the other side based on gestures of parity management, rank matching, and reaching agreements through dialogue and consultation gave rise to a third relational practice: IDF officers often acted as go-betweens, mediating agents between the movement and political actors. Combined, these relational practices and routines effectively established underbidding.

Importantly, however, there was nothing inevitable about this development. In the wake of the Sebastia campaign, the evolution of underbidding saw meaningful challenges. Partly indicative of challenges to the movement's strategic bargaining position (i.e., unfavorable opportunity spirals), this was the case because the government and the prime minister often disapproved of what they saw as over-discretion on the part of IDF senior officers, consistent with both their personal and professional positions. Prime Minister Yitzak Rabin's disapproval of CGS Gur's role and approach was a case in point (Shifris 2013). Another (discussed in Section 1) involved Minister of Defense Ezer Weitzman's dismissal of CGS Rafael Eitan's attempt to work out a compromise during the confrontation in Rujeib in September 1979.

Underbidding was also challenged because some movement leaders and activists failed to realize or refused to accept the unique positionality and role of the IDF. During the spring of 1976, tension mounted between the military government and settler leaders in the Palestinian West Bank city of Hebron, where a settlement had existed since 1968 (see Section 3). The tension related to the increase in Palestinian attacks on Jewish property that accompanied the Palestinian municipality elections taking place. Instead of working with heads of the military government, settlers acted independently and violently against Palestinians. Following the elections, settler leaders bypassed the military governor and tried unsuccessfully to work with Minister of Defense Shimon

Peres to arrange reconciliation with the elected mayor of Hebron. They later realized their failure was related to the military governor's decision to block correspondence between them and Peres (Sprinzak Interview Collection, April 1986).

3.2.1 Underbidding Consolidated

Despite this rocky road, the relational practices and routines between the movement and the IDF consolidated. This development stood in contrast to the relationship between the movement and the police, which was characterized by unwillingness on the part of the latter to engage in any negotiation with settler groups and to exercise an escalated force style of policing. Nowhere was this more apparent than during the weeks of protest activity surrounding the final ratification of the Camp David Accords (March 23, 1979), which met heavy repression, including an unprecedented round of preemptive arrests and the use of a special counterterrorism unit of the Border Guard police force (Sprinzak 1991; author's data).

The consolidation of underbidding occurred most meaningfully during the last stages of the struggle against the destruction of Yammit and prevented more lethal violence. Given restrictions on the presence of reporters on site, we have little information in the press on the events unfolding during that last week. Nevertheless, a first-hand account (bolstered by transcripts of the radio communication network connecting the various loci of struggle during that week) offered by a member of the Jewish Underground (Segal 1999) is revealing. Alongside highly detailed descriptions of confrontations between resisters and evacuators, some of which developed into outright violence, we are also told about the constructive, moderating role of the IDF and how it ultimately put a brake on much higher levels of violence. In sharp contrast to the police, and even more so the Border Guard forces, IDF officers, including the commander of the Southern Command and CGS Eitan, repeatedly exercised discretion and prevented higher levels of violence. At times, this discretion was in response to immediate situations, as with CGS Eitan's decision to remove the blockade imposed abruptly on the Rafiah Salient after talking with MHRS leaders and sensing the level of anger. When reprimanded by Prime Minister Begin for expressing doubts about the directives of the political echelon, "CGS Eitan asked if the Prime Minister thought he should resign" (Segal 1999: 67). At other times, discretion was more general, reflecting an approach that went beyond, and at times against, directives, and involved insistence on coordination and engagement in contact and dialogue with the opposition. As an IDF colonel revealed, "I was fully convinced that closeness and developing familiarity and friendship between soldiers and residents would prove useful when eviction time comes" (Ibid. 304).

3.2.2 Underbidding under Strain: The First Intifada

The post-Yammit period saw a further strengthening of the convergence of interests and values between the IDF and the movement. As part of a decision to reduce IDF presence in the Occupied Territories, made in the wake of the Yammit debacle and shortly after the outbreak of the Lebanon War (June 1982), the ADS system was expanded to include special battalions. These battalions, manned by settlers, were assigned to policing and routine security tasks. In practical terms, this meant that they were solely responsible for routine security inside and outside the settlements. Additionally, these battalions were staffed mainly by soldiers who lived in the settlements and were armed with higher quality and far more sophisticated weaponry than before. Finally, the ADS system's growing security value and the settlement population's expanding presence led to a greater demand for settlers to be more actively involved in shaping IDF policy. This resulted in the formation of a battalions' security committee that routinely informed the IDF of emerging needs and demands. As of late 1982, representatives of that committee began to participate in IDF senior command operational meetings.

These developments notwithstanding, underbidding faced continued challenges, which began to cumulate throughout the mid-1980s and culminated during the first Palestinian Intifada, which lasted from 1987 to early 1993 (see Box 2). The Intifada was an exceptionally strained period in the relationship between the IDF and the movement for two reasons. The first related to the increase in the quantity and quality of Palestinian attacks. Though instances of Palestinian acts of aggression against settlers and settlers' retaliatory, vengeful attacks had become a constant feature before 1987 (Weisburd 1989), the Intifada saw an exponential increase in the frequency and intensity of these attacks. This increase led to greater demands on the part of settlers for more security and a much stricter law-and-order policy to salvage the settlement enterprise. According to Zertal and Eldar, the Intifada brought about a dramatic decrease in demand for housing in the area. In fact, they argue that movement leaders considered it the "toughest challenge since the beginning of the settlement enterprise" (2004: 143–144).

The second reason the first Intifada was such a strained period related to the presence of Israeli progressive forces and, more broadly, divisions in Israeli society concerning the Occupied Territories and resolution of the conflict. With the IDF a people's army, it was expected that such divisions would filter into its

<table>
<tr><td colspan="2" align="center">Box 2 Key dates and actors: First Intifada</td></tr>
<tr><td>April 11, 1987</td><td>Israel Foreign Minister Peres and King Hussein of Jordan try to promote a framework for peace</td></tr>
<tr><td>June 6</td><td>Clashes between settlers, Palestinians, and IDF forces in Dheisheh refugee camp; Peace rallies of Israeli progressive groups in Tel Aviv and Jerusalem</td></tr>
<tr><td>December 9</td><td>Palestinian uprising (Intifada) begins in full force</td></tr>
<tr><td>February 1988</td><td>Secretary-General of the YESHA Council if forced to resign</td></tr>
<tr><td>March 24</td><td>First attack of a newly formed underground group called Sicarii</td></tr>
<tr><td>October 5</td><td>Israel's Central Elections Committee bans *Kach* party</td></tr>
<tr><td>November 11</td><td>General elections in Israel; A second unity government between Likud and Alignment</td></tr>
<tr><td>December 14</td><td>Opening of American-Palestine Liberation Organization dialogue</td></tr>
<tr><td>January 18, 1989</td><td>Establishment of the State of Judea</td></tr>
<tr><td>April 14</td><td>Prime Minister Shamir proposes an election plan for the Occupied Territories as a first step toward Palestinian self-rule</td></tr>
<tr><td>June 11, 1990</td><td>Prime Minister Shamir forms a new right-wing coalition</td></tr>
<tr><td>October 8</td><td>Massive clashes on the Temple Mount, resulting in the death of 19 Palestinians and injury of 180 Palestinians and 20 Israelis</td></tr>
<tr><td>October 30, 1991</td><td>International Peace Conference in Madrid; start of bilateral Israeli-Arab peace talks in Washington</td></tr>
<tr><td>June 23, 1992</td><td>Yitzhak Rabin-led Labor victory in the national elections</td></tr>
<tr><td>December 16</td><td>Deportation of hundreds of Hamas and Palestinian Islamic Jihad activists to Lebanon</td></tr>
</table>

ranks, low and senior alike. The division between Right and Left was also not new, stretching back to the results of the June 1967 War. At times, the intensity of the divide had tragic consequences (e.g., the killing of a leftwing activist by a grenade thrown by a rightwing activist at a peace rally against the Lebanon War). Nevertheless, the Intifada engendered sharper ideological boundaries between the moderate Left and the hardline Right (Arian and Ventura 1989). Moreover, once the Palestinian action strategy of restricted violence became clear, it also brought about an increase in Israeli leftwing opposition to the Israeli government's counter-insurgency policy (Kaminer 1996; Herman 2009; Cohen 2019). Worse still in the eyes of the movement, were initiatives by moderate settler figures who called for the rebuilding of bridges with leftwing groups and those who suggested meeting and talking with the PLO (Eldar and Zertal 2004).

Separately and jointly, these heightened interactions between movement actors and Palestinian activists and between movement actors and Israeli progressive activists injected tremendous tension into underbidding. What had been sporadic instances of refusal on the part of radical settler groups to follow IDF orders, on the one hand, and the unwillingness of IDF officers to manage interactions with settler activists through dialogue, on the other, became more frequent. An example took place in early August 1986, when repeated, forceful attempts of a group of ultra-radical Bloc settlers to break through IDF checkpoints to reach an ancient synagogue in Jericho eventually resulted in soldiers shooting and hitting the settlers' vehicle (*Yediot Achronot*, August 8, 1986). Later, when the Intifada consolidated, settler groups took the law into their own hands when their demands for restoring safety and order were unmet or met in ways they perceived as inadequate. They formed special vigilante units and initiated retaliatory, punitive raids on Palestinian villages, towns, and refugee camps. Instances of settlers refusing to disperse when ordered to do so by the IDF force on site, actively resisting arrest, or beating soldiers and officers began to cumulate.

A telling case took place in early June 1987, when a vigilante group called the Committee for the Safety of the Roads, comprising of *Kach* activists, decided that a Palestinian stoning of a bus just outside Jerusalem that injured a Kiryat Arba settler should not go unpunished. Arriving at the Dheisheh Refugee Camp near Bethlehem, they began firing in the air. Quickly enough, the residents surrounded the advancing groups and violent brawls erupted. "IDF forces arrived at the camp to end the confrontation and were surprised when members of the Committee . . . began lashing out at them as well, refusing to leave the site. The soldiers were finally forced to use tear gas to drive the activists out of the refugee camp" (Pedahzur and Perliger 2009: 91). Several days later, when some of the settlers who were arrested stood trial, the complete and worrisome details of the event were revealed. It appeared that the settlers not only brutally attacked the IDF battalion commander, a reserve officer, but also, during their escape, hit and injured one of the soldiers with their car (Eldar and Zertal 2004).

Hardly a coincidence, the attack in Dheisheh took place on the same day that Israeli progressive groups, including Peace Now and Israeli Arab activists, organized peace rallies in Tel Aviv and Jerusalem, calling for an end to twenty years of occupation. The peace rally in Jerusalem was met by a counter-demonstration organized by rightwing and settler activists. After the latter's' several attempts to disrupt the rally, the police stepped in and instructed them to disperse. Their refusal resulted in a violent clash with the police. The counter-demonstration in Jerusalem and many others like it became indicative of a general sense of alarm by movement actors in light of the wave of pro-peace events, moves, and initiatives organized not only by non-institutional forces but also by (and with) institutional actors.

3.3 Disintegrating Underbidding and Radicalization

In this context of reinvigorated peace activism, a clandestine organization was formed.[20] The underground group – named after the Jewish zealot Sicarii rebels during the time of ancient Rome – involved activists from *Kach* and other ultra-radical groups who targeted known Israeli leftwing and other public figures, including moderate rightwing ones who expressed pro-peace opinions. Between early 1988 and June 1990, the organization sent threatening letters, initiated nine reported terrorist attacks against public figures, and bombed the property of well-known individuals (Sprinzak Media Collection; Pedahzur and Perliger 2009; Author's data).

The growing salience of flanking and polarization and the ensuing instances of radicalization took place in the context of the disintegration of underbidding and the unprecedented fragmentation and rift at the movement level. The movement was torn into different camps, each claiming to represent the genuine goals of the movement and the proper strategy and tactics for their realization. The coalition of ultra-radical forces formed during the struggle against the eviction of Yammit turned into the most influential camp, took over the Bloc, and declared itself the authentic leadership of the Settlement Movement. It became so popular that its members enjoyed the support of leadership figures and other central activists in various institutions and organizations of the movement and among Israelis in general. Rabbi Kahane's *Kach* became influential enough to win a seat in the Knesset during the 1984 general elections, and its popularity continued to soar. When the Secretary-General of the YESHA Council criticized their repeated attempts to forcefully break through the IDF

---

[20] A second clandestine organization, less impactful and lasting, was DOV (a play on the Hebrew acronym of *Dikui Bogdim* – suppression of traitors) (Pedazur and Perliger 2009; Alimi and Hirsch-Hoefler 2012).

checkpoint in Jericho (see above), he was accused of stabbing them in the back and was called on to resign (*Yediot*, August 11, 1986). The internal rebellion of the ultra-radicals culminated in February 1988 when the Secretary-General was impeached (Harnoy 1994).

The disintegration of underbidding was also related to the noticeable weakening of the movement's bargaining position vis-à-vis the political establishment. Despite previous inroads into the Israeli political establishment – about which we say more in the Section 3 – the movement experienced meaningful setbacks to its ability to generate input into the policymaking process. This was primarily the result of the stalemate resulting from the 1984 elections, which led to the formation of two successive unity governments under the joint leadership of the two main parties, Alignment and Likud. The first government, 1984–1988, had Alignment leader Shimon Peres at the helm, rotating the prime minister post with Likud leader Yizhak Shamir in 1986, and the second government, 1988–1991, had no rotation with Shamir at the helm throughout its tenure.

Even when Alignment leader Peres was no longer prime minister, as was the case following the rotation of October 1986, there was little the movement could achieve. In 1985, the settlement enterprise was forced to go on a drastic diet, with hardly any new settlements built. In July 1985, the Knesset passed legislation (initiated by Alignment MKs) that would disqualify Kahane's *Kach* party from running for the Knesset in October 1988. Following the rotation, when the Likud's Shamir became prime minister, Alignment ministers remained in central and influential positions. Peres became minister of finance and, as acting prime minister, was exceptionally active in initiating pro-peace plans (e.g., the attempt to promote a framework for peace with Jordan, known as the London Agreement of April 1987).

The Intifada also put Israel on the defensive internationally, with unprecedented scrutiny of its settlement policy and increasing pressure on Prime Minister Shamir to consider a political settlement vis-à-vis the Palestinian leadership. Following the disqualification of *Kach* and in light of international recognition of the Palestinian Liberation Organization, the PLO, in November 1988, *Kach* members, as well as supporters from additional ultra-radical elements, decided to disengage from the State of Israel. In January 1989, they declared the establishment of the independent "State of Judea" as a fully *Halakhic* Jewish State to be located in the southern areas of the West Bank (Sprinzak 1991; Pedahzur and Perliger 2009). Even though the initiative did not materialize, it did receive the support of key figures and groups that were part of the Bloc, including respected rabbis. Moreover, evidence suggesting that Prime Minister Shamir was caving to pressure in April 1989 and was set to propose an election plan for the Occupied Territories as part of a peaceful settlement and future self-rule, brought about a surge of settler violence (Waller 1990; Eldar and Zertal 2004).

3.3.1 Attempts at Restoring Underbidding

A useful way to demonstrate how relational dynamics mediate the influence of polarization and flanking and, in turn, specify the possibility of radicalization is by offering an exception that proves the rule. This exception relates to the approach of the head of the Central Command, Major-General Amnon Mitzna, vis-à-vis movement actors, which proved successful in restoring underbidding and putting a brake on radicalization, even if only in part. Mitzna began serving as commander in May 1987 (shortly before the events in the Dheisheh Refugee Camp) and held that position for two years. Despite initial suspicion on the part of several settler leaders who were involved in Yammit and remembered his strict approach, they gradually came to appreciate his style of command, which combined practicality and consideration.

His approach involved direct, personal ties and ongoing contact and dialogue, and led to understandings and expectations regarding unacceptable forms and types of behavior by both sides. It rested on earnest efforts to get to know the settler population and its leadership, its different types, groupings, and ideological nuances. Realizing how reluctant Minister of Defense Rabin and the Chief of General Staff were to meet with settler leaders, yet enjoying their full backing, Mitzna delivered the message that the Central Command was not just responsible for the settler population, acting when necessary as their go-between with the government. Mitzna took things one step further and made it clear that the head of the Central Command was the only source of authority to turn to and that it would be wrong and futile to try and influence IDF decisions indirectly via the political echelon. Moreover, fully aware of the extreme elements within the movement, Mitzna began to "support those with whom you could talk." According to Mitzna, it was not about giving settlers what they wanted, but essentially about assisting and offering support vis-à-vis the provision of services related to security and transportation and lending a hand with specific concerns and issues (e.g., further adjustment to the *Yeshivot Hesder* framework – discussed in the next section) (*Yediot*, July 1989, p. 71; personal conversation with Mitzna, January 29, 2023).

As it turned out, no matter how effective Mitzna's efforts to restore relations and trust proved to be, there was only so much these efforts could achieve without reinforcing developments unfolding among movement actors and between the movement and political authorities. For example, establishing a more explicit set of rules and understandings with the more pragmatic leaders of the movement required complementary efforts at coordination among elements within the movement, which were either absent or unsuccessful. For a while, the fall of the unity government in Spring 1990 and the formation of a rightwing ruling coalition in June 1990 brought with it some improvement in the bargaining position of the movement. The new government, headed by the Likud's Shamir, promoted a more proactive settlement policy and exercised harsher repressive measures against Palestinians, as expressed in the cycle of violence on the Temple Mount in October 1990. This improvement in the political leverage of the movement, however, was too brief given the tremendous pressure put on Israel by world powers to enter negotiations with Palestinian delegates at the Madrid Peace Conference in November 1991, to the outrage of the movement.

3.4 Underbidding in the Gaza Pullout

Certain developments during the 1990s stressed an already strained pattern of interaction between the movement and Israeli security forces even further. If the first Intifada deepened the domestic division among Israelis concerning the "Territories issue," it became even sharper following the implementation stages of what became known as the Oslo Peace Accords of September 1993. Just as the IDF, a socially and politically embedded institution, could not remain isolated entirely from politics during the first Intifada, it was equally, if not more deeply, involved in preparing for and implementing the peace accords. Similar to its impact on Prime Minister Rabin's thinking, the first Intifada engendered a shift in the geopolitical and geostrategic thinking of the General Staff regarding the Israeli-Arab conflict. This shift involved recognition of the existence of a distinct Palestinian nation, hence a separate actor, possibly a partner for peace (Peri 2006).

One issue emerging from such a shift was the widespread stance against the notion of "territories for peace" among movement actors and the settlement population more broadly. This was a significant problem because the IDF, as a citizens' army based on reserve duty, needed to take the stances and opinions of many diverse social groups and sectors into consideration in forging and executing policy (Peri 2006; Levy 2007). The gradually increasing value of movement actors and the settlement population to the IDF strengthened further following the introduction in 1988 of a consequential addition to the *Yeshivot Hesder* framework. This addition took the form of "pre-military preparatory colleges" that strengthened graduates' religious affiliations and encouraged them to enlist in elite fighting units and join the officer track (Cohen 1999).

Indeed, if the overall proportion of Religious-Zionist soldiers in regular combat units amounted to several percent during the 1980s, during the early 2000s, that portion reached 25–30 percent (Levy 2014).

When a second Intifada (named Al-Aqsa) erupted in October 2000, the value of the settlement population to the IDF was far more meaningful than before. Heads of the IDF and the movement were fully aware of this and recognized the volatile situation and its inherent risks. The second round of Palestinian Intifada differed most strikingly from the first in the severity and lethality of violent attacks (i.e., heavy reliance on terrorist attacks, including suicide terrorism) and the intensity and scope of such attacks (i.e., spilling over into almost every Israeli city, town, and settlement on a daily basis). These features pushed forward a process of closing ranks and rallying around the flag on the Israeli side (Feinstein 2022). While not disappearing altogether, the Israeli peace movement lost much of its mainstream and mass-based features (Cohen 2019).

Nevertheless, the Al-Aqsa Intifada pushed Israel to adopt a unilateral policy, which began to take shape in June 2002 as a "separation barrier" and developed into a plan to pullout from the Gaza Strip in December 2003. To senior IDF officers, it was clear that putting religious soldiers, particularly settler soldiers and officers, in situations in stark contradiction to their value systems might lead to wide-scale disobedience, desertion, or even rebellion. To movement leaders, it was clear that an outright confrontation with and break from the IDF would constitute a profound crisis with far-reaching consequences (Haloutz 2010). First, mutual recognition of the ominous links between the IDF's role in the Pullout, the chances of widespread disobedience, and large-scale violence were related to the heightened friction between movement actors and security forces throughout the country, including in the Occupied Territories.[21] It also related to ultra-radical extremist elements within the movement and the unfavorable, threat-inducing developments unfolding in the political arena. Finally, it related to the adverse effects of intensifying, and at times worsening, Palestinian actions in the form of property and bodily damage, terrorist attacks, and missile firings on settlements.

3.4.1 The Disobedience Dilemma

There is no question that Prime Minister Ariel Sharon's decision to put the IDF in charge of carrying out the Pullout (with the assistance of the police) heightened tension between the contending parties. Despite practical and logistical

---

[21] Police presence in the West Bank broadened following the horrendous massacre at the Cave of the Patriarchs by a far-right *Kach* activist in February 1994. We return to this tragic event in Section Three.

justifications, pertaining, for example, to the necessary pooling of resources, it was clear to all that Sharon had a strategic consideration as well. Knowing how valued and esteemed the IDF was among the predominantly Religious-Zionist settlement population, Sharon hoped that putting the army in charge of the operation rather than the police would minimize the potential for violence despite the sensitivity and risk involved. Indeed, the Pullout brought to the fore with full intensity the tension between two central sets of values: the State of Israel and its institutions, and the Greater Israel. This tension brought to the surface issues that centered on the conditions under which disobedience was permitted and, once allowed, its acceptable types (selective or collective) and forms (passive or active).

Movement leaders thought Sharon used the IDF instrumentally and somewhat manipulatively. When a leader of GKAC was asked about the reasoning behind the government's decision to use the IDF rather than considering alternatives, such as putting the police in charge, he revealed: "After all, all of us served or are serving in the IDF. How, then, could we raise arms on soldiers? The military is different from the police … the military is not something you join voluntarily and treat as a profession. We were angered by the decision to use the army … it is part of our being and identity and was used in a highly questionable way."

The deepening tension between the two value systems led some to call on soldiers and officers to disobey orders. In petitions, opinion pieces, and pamphlets, it was argued that any order designed to evict Jews from their homes was illegal and anti-*Halakhic*. It was explicitly argued that all it would take for the IDF to be incapable of carrying out the Pullout was to have soldiers from all *Yeshivot Hesder* and pre-military religious colleges state their refusal to follow the eviction order. To bolster their calls, these forces managed to secure the cooperation and signatures of several ultra-radical rabbis on a petition calling for IDF soldiers to disobey, circulated in late 2004. However, it was the call of Rabbi Avraham Shapira, one of the most influential rabbis at the time, in April 2005, that alarmed the movement leadership and the IDF command.

In response to Rabbi Shapira's call, the field leadership of the movement and other more pragmatic and moderate rabbis sought to soften his call for disobedience without undermining his spiritual authority. They did that by offering their interpretation, according to which Rabbi Shapira's call did not constitute a sweeping call for disobedience, but rather referred to individual soldiers. Despite internal opposition from within the movement voiced by leaders of the ultra-radical organizations, it became clear that leaders of the "primary victim" – residents of Gush Katif – were adamantly against disobedience as part of their staunch integrationist approach. The conscious decision made by leaders of GKAC was to object to any expression of disobedience and, even more forcefully, attacks on the security forces. Even when the Pullout loomed large, on June 30, 2005, following several incidents of damage to IDF property inside Gush Katif by settler activists who were not locals, the main article in the GKAC newsletter, titled "Even Orange does not Cross Red Lines" read as follow:

> One of the key features of moral struggle is the existence of red lines that should not be crossed no matter the situation. In light of the events of last week, we felt it was necessary to restate the following: We happily welcome those who come and join us to bolster the struggle. We expect our guests to behave in good manners that respect us while here . . . [P]hysical, even verbal attack on the body and dignity of IDF soldiers is . . . out of the question under any circumstances. We fear that certain elements are interested in painting the residents of Gush Katif in ways that do not represent who they truly are, thus undermining the broad public support the Gush enjoys. We must not lend a hand to this move.

Although the critical mass of movement activists and adherents was against disobedience, the hope shared by many was that there would be enough soldiers and officers who would not obey the eviction order. Despite such hope, or perhaps precisely because of it, leaders of the movement and heads of the IDF and police were aware of the highly volatile situation. They acted according to their joint interest to prevent violence and minimize the potential for radicalization.

3.4.2 Developing Rules of Engagement

It is one thing to recognize an exceptionally high potential for violence and the mutual interest in dealing with it. Acting on this mutual recognition and interest in curbing that potential and containing its manifestations is another thing. Heads of the IDF and the police worked systematically with leaders of the Council and GKAC to establish and maintain a clear set of rules of engagement based on understandings and expectations regarding the legitimate and accept-able scale, form, and scope of contention and repression. This was translated into several meaningful practices and routines that built on past ones, yet included important nuances from lessons learned:

1. Systematic acts to preserve the legitimacy of the Council and GKAC vis-à-vis their public: The IDF command was concerned that a drop in the leadership's legitimacy would create a power vacuum that ultra-radical groups would fill, hence the greater likelihood of violence. To this end, IDF senior officers acted to support the leadership's standing in several ways: (a) Making sure to hold routine meetings with their representatives for briefings and information

exchange and disclosing some of them to their relevant publics; (b) creating a leadership equilibrium vis-à-vis the Council, such that senior officers holding at least the rank of brigade commander would participate in all meetings; (c) greater willingness to approve the Council's requests for building permits in settlements; and (d) returning firearms to specific individuals based on requests for special permits made by the Council and GKAC, even after a large-scale operation for the collection of weaponry had been carried out.

2. Systematic activity to reduce the disobedience potential based on designated, ongoing workshops for soldiers and officers on the meaning of disobedience, its various types and forms, how to minimize it, and how to deal with it in actual encounters. Along these lines, specific decisions were made; for example, to reduce the involvement of soldiers from the special frameworks (e.g., pre-military religious colleges) in the pending evacuation and prevent soldiers who were residents of evacuated settlements from participating.

3. Conducting routine meetings with rabbis from across the board and all regions, including those from West Bank and Gaza Strip settlements, Israel's chief rabbis, and heads of the special frameworks, to deliberate and discuss ongoing and emerging issues and problems.

The mutual interest to avoid violent collision led to an understanding on the part of the General Staff that it was necessary to allow movement actors to express their discontent while also working behind the scenes to preserve coordination on an ongoing basis. One of the interviewees, a high-ranking IDF officer in the Central Command, offered a glimpse into how some of the above practices and routines developed:

> There often were informal and unspoken rules. For example, we made it clear that passive resistance is okay but never harming soldiers. From their side, we sensed how apprehensive they were about the presence of YASAM forces [equivalent to SWAT teams], and so we agreed to the request of the YESHA Council to minimize the involvement of these units as much as possible and worked with the police to make that happen.

The movement leadership played a complementary role. The words of one interviewee from GKAC, in charge of ongoing security tasks in the Gush Katif region, are instructive because they reveal something about the mutually benefitting symbiotic relationship between settlers and local IDF forces. When asked to clarify what he meant by working with the IDF, he said, "We constantly updated each other, and there were instances of tactical coordination. When a group of extremists infiltrated into Gush Katif and took over an abandoned hotel and began to attack Palestinians, we broke into the hotel, took over their weapons, and told the IDF forces to step in."

The police contributed to ongoing coordination with the leadership of the movement. However, they were also forced to take a far more active role than was anticipated, one that resembled the traditional mediating role of the IDF. This was particularly so in the weeks before the Pullout began when the police was faced with little guidance from the government regarding how to deal with the skyrocketing number of protest events throughout the country. According to a high-ranking police officer:

> It was a like a "game" with a predetermined set of rules. Even after Kfar Mymon [the "connection march" – see Introduction] we allowed additional mass rallies realizing it was critical for making them look potent … that they were doing things, a sort of ventilation. We allowed all forms of protest as long as there would be no violence … at the end of the day, if the other side's leadership is effective, then you should work with it and strengthen it. Having someone you can talk to serves you well. The government knew about this type of interaction, and we got its backing, yet there was this kind of disconnect developing between them and Sharon's government, especially in the months before the evacuation, and we had to walk into this vacuum and look for ways to fill it.

The patterns that emerge from plotting data on the level and form of contention and repression and the number of Palestinian rocket firings for one month after three critical events (Figure 6) validate the preceding analysis of the operation and the effects of underbidding.

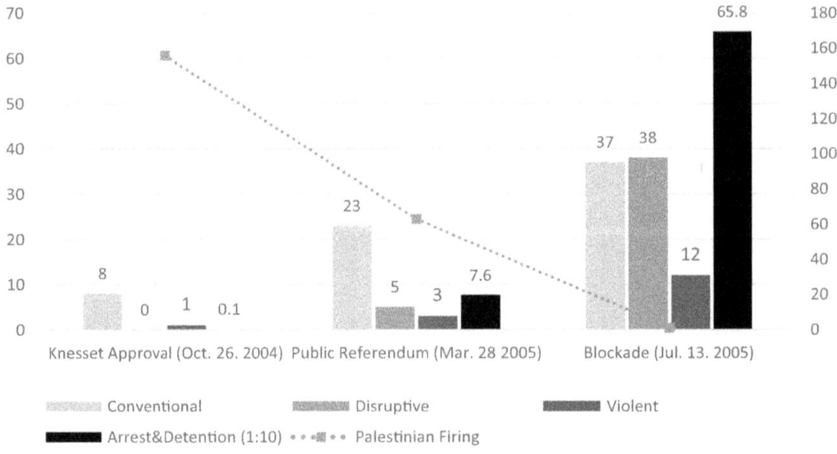

Figure 6 Level and form of settler contention, security forces repression, and Palestinian rocket firings

Source: Author's Data

Three points are worth noting. First, despite the mounting tension and increase in contentious activity, the level of government repression is more closely related to a rise in the general level of contention than to a rise in violent forms of contention. This is evident following the fall of the Public Referendum Bill and, even more so, the imposition of the Blockade. It also seems that most instances of settler violence against Palestinians (and settler violence more generally) took place following these two events, when occurrences of Palestinian rocket fire were dropping, if not approximating zero.

The other two points relate to what the numbers cannot tell. Of the sixteen instances of settler violence, only one was directed at the Israeli-Jewish general population; it involved throwing stones at vehicles on July 19, 2005. This finding is revealing, particularly given the presence of institutional and non-institutional groups that were pro-Pullout and whose activity increased during June and July of 2005. Most of the other violent incidents were directed at IDF and police forces and property either because movement activists were prevented from entering the Gaza Strip or because members of the security forces experienced backlash for trying to stop attacks on Palestinians.

The willingness and ability of the movement leadership and heads of the Israeli security forces to establish and maintain underbidding unquestionably played a central role in containing radicalization. The influences of cognitive and environmental mechanisms were also mitigated as a result. In addition, it is clear that the moderating effect of underbidding on the level of settler violence shaped, and was shaped by, the ability of the central leadership of the movement to form and sustain consensus mobilization. However, the combined effect of these two relational mechanisms on containing radicalization during the Gaza Pullout campaign was contingent upon the facilitating operation and influence of opportunity spirals – which is the topic of Section 3.

4 Movement–Authorities and Opportunity Spirals

The third framework of relational dynamics for understanding processes of contained radicalization involves interactions between social movements and the political establishment. Rejecting the dichotomy between prescribed and non-prescribed politics, the following analysis centers on changes in the structure of political opportunities and threats, and treats them as essentially relational (Meyer and Tarrow 1998; McAdam and Tarrow 2010; Meyer 2021). These changes reflect shifts in connections and ties between the complex sets of actors that constitute both social movements and the political establishment (McAdam 1999; McAdam et al. 2001; Goldstone 2004). The mechanism of opportunity spirals captures the complex and multifaceted dynamics between the sides and focuses on the ability of movement leadership to exert political leverage based on a solid bargaining position.

Most scholars of Israeli society and politics agree that the Settlement Movement is the most influential social movement in Israel's history. The movement, however, did not always enjoy a bargaining position that enabled it to exert political leverage, and not all state policies relevant to the movement's agenda were beneficial or constructive to its goals. A central driver in the ascendence of the movement and, importantly, the process of contained radicalization, relates to the history of relation-building between the movement and the Israeli political establishment. As with the mechanisms analyzed in previous sections, the emergence and evolution of opportunity spirals was neither linear nor determinate, and it was interrelated with concomitant relational dynamics unfolding at the intra-movement level and between it and the IDF. When this coevolution of relational mechanisms became mutually reinforcing, it impeded the influence of cognitive and environmental drivers and contained radicalization.

4.1 The Emergence of Opportunity Spirals

The emergence of opportunity spirals between the movement and the Israeli political establishment began immediately following the June 1967 War. It rested on relational practices and routines that were part of the cultural style that characterized the Israeli political regime long before and well after statehood. Central to these regime features were an instrumental orientation toward the rule of law, favoritism, and a general approach to politics that favored arrangements, accommodations, and compromises (Zisser and Cohen 1999). Fully aware of these features, leaders of the movement capitalized on several relational practices and routines, three of which became central. The first is tie activation, which is about the activation of connection with specific individuals with personal ties to powerholders[22]; the second is brokerage, which is about the linking of two or more parties or social sites by a third party who derives some benefit from the connection (McAdam et al. 2001); and the third is building cross-sectoral alliances with as many political forces as possible. While not necessarily having a coherent strategy and not without erring and subsequently making necessary adjustments, settler activists were quick to realize the effectiveness of these practices and routines for developing a powerful bargaining position for the movement, hence increasing its ability to exercise political leverage.

---

[22] The common expression in Israel at the time was *krovim la'malkhut*, which translates to "close to the throne".

The process began to develop shortly after the June 1967 War in the context of a settlement drive that was either initiated or approved by the government. For example, the ability of members of the settlement nucleus to arrange for private meetings with the most influential powerholders at the time made the settlement initiative of Kfar Etzion (launched in July 1967) a success story. Disappointed by the tepid position of their political representatives – the National Religious Party (NRP), the party of the religious-Zionist public – nucleus members approached known figures from the Land of Israel Movement (LIM), the first organized group of the Settlement Movement. Aware of the famous and highly influential public figures involved in LIM, nucleus members asked them to use their connections with top-level politicians to promote their cause. Within weeks, they managed to gain the support of the most influential members of the cabinet, including Minister of Defense Moshe Dayan and Prime Minister Levi Eshkol (Shiloah 1989; Admoni 1992; Zertal and Eldar 2004). Later, in April 1968, the group of settlers who initiated the Hebron settlement (named Kiryat Arba) had ample allies acting on their behalf with and without the involvement of acknowledged intermediaries. On top of brokering efforts taken by opposition and ruling coalition members, the vigorous involvement of the Minister of Labor and soon-to-be Deputy Prime Minister Yigal Allon made a difference. Driven in part by his competition with Minister of Defense Dayan over the leadership of the Alignment Party, Allon's support went as far as providing the settlers with weapons and played a pivotal role in the approval of the settlement (Pedatzur 1996; Huberman 2008).

The emergence of opportunity spirals broadened to include cross-sectional alliance-building during the initiative to build a settlement in the northern part of the West Bank *against* government-declared policy – the Sebastia campaign of June 1974 and December 1975. The defiant character of this settlement initiative rendered the practice of building cross-sectoral alliances with as many political forces as possible particularly important. It offered the movement a broader pool of meaningful connections, potential brokers, and, critically, much-needed maneuvering space. Indeed, the gradually built alliance included not just those political parties with which the movement had a certain degree of ideological or instrumental common ground (respectively, the ruling coalition partner NRP and the main opposition party Likud). It also included representatives from other parties and factions for whom the Territories were of utmost importance for political or security reasons, as was the case with representatives from certain factions of the ruling Alignment party.

Efforts to form alliances were rooted in the realization of most movement actors that convergence of interests or values was insufficient for developing a robust enough bargaining position. It was well understood, for example, that changes in the set of opportunities and constraints of a given ally might lead to divergence instead of convergence. Settler leaders realized that their movement could reach out to many party actors and dissociate itself from any single party – as indeed happened in the spring of 1974 when the Bloc broke away from NRP. So earnest was such belief in non-partisanship that even when the extraordinarily popular support of the movement became evident, ideas to form a new political party were unequivocally rejected (Zertal and Eldar 2004).

That realization also meant engaging in relation work directly with representatives of political parties and indirectly via their social bases. According to Rubinstein (1982), during the spring and summer of 1974, movement leaders and key activists held numerous meetings and talks with cabinet ministers, Knesset members, and machine politicians (p. 72; see also Huberman 2008). The breadth and depth of the alliance formed is apparent from the words of Minister of Defense Peres in a meeting of Alignment held shortly after the Sebastia Compromise of December 1975. Responding to accusations that the Compromise undermined the authority of the government in failing to enforce the law, Peres reacted fervently, stating, "It was not just Gush Emunim in Sebastia ... there were colonists from all streams, from Ha'kibbutz Ha'Meukhad (United Kibbutz), Union of Groups and Kibbutzim, Ha'Kibbutz Ha'hartzi (the National Kibbutz) and the Cooperative Colonizing Movement" (Zertal and Eldar 2004: 75 – additions by author).[23] But it was not just among members of Alignment that the movement gained sympathy and traction: Movement activists made similar approaches to rightwing parties, including the Likud and NRP. Revealingly, relation work with Likud was led by a small group of LIM members, who were also affiliated with various elements of Alignment (Shiloah 1989).

4.1.1 Opportunity Spirals at Play

Combined with an impressive pool of ties to use and brokers to rely on, such a cross-party alliance not only made the fifteen-month-long Sebastia campaign possible, but also facilitated the establishment of a strong bargaining position that enabled the movement to exert meaningful pressure on the government. With influential members of his cabinet either willing to come to terms with or actively supporting the settlement initiative, and many known politicians and representatives from all parties coming to Sebastia to express their support, Prime Minister Rabin was forced to consider a compromise. Around the same

---

[23] Each "camp" or grouping of the broad Zionist Movement had distinctive social and political institutions, clubs, and colonizing bodies. Broadly speaking, Alignment was associated with the socialist-oriented "Labor camp" and Likud with the liberalist-oriented "Revisionist camp."

time that Minister of Defense Peres was informing the settlers they needed to disperse and that the government would hold a special meeting to rethink its settlement policy in the region, Rabin accepted a compromise. Tellingly, the compromise proposal was brought to him by a personal acquaintance, Haim Gouri, a well-known journalist and a member of LIM. Gouri's proposal was based on talks he held with settler leaders in Sebastia and informal consultations with several members of the government (*Yediot Achronot*, December 12, 1975, p. 3; December 16, 1975, p. 16). The final version of the compromise proposal was deliberated on with settler leaders together with Rabin's defense advisor Ariel Sharon (at the time, a member of Likud and an earnest supporter of the settlement enterprise).

What was meaningful about the Sebastia compromise had little to do with its content (i.e., relocation of thirty families to a nearby military base and the promise of a more permanent location in the future). The significance of the compromise related to the process through which it was reached and the essence of what was achieved. Specifically, it was the first time the movement had held a sufficiently strong bargaining position, allowing it to seize and create opportunities to advance its agenda. It was also the first time such an advancement entailed a change in declared governmental policy against establishing settlements in densely populated Palestinian areas of the West Bank.

Of equal importance was the way opportunity spirals operated solely and jointly with consensus mobilization and underbidding and put a brake on radicalization. In light of the violent and secretive features of most previous operations to settle Sebastia, some of which involved settler violence, the seventh operation (November 25, 1975) and particularly the last one of early December were different. Not only were they conducted in the open, but they were also predominantly nonviolent. When Minister of Defense Peres told movement leaders that he came to the site to demand their unconditional dispersal, signs of unrest among the crowd induced the commander of the Central Command to instruct the IDF forces surrounding the area to close ranks and prepare for an attack. Leaders of the movement, however, were quick to step in and inform the commander of their intention to take control of the situation, which they did, and effectively so (Huberman 2008: 107; see also *Yediot Achronot*, December 8, 1975, p. 3). Further consolidating the dynamics of mutual reinforcement between the three relational mechanisms were the systematic efforts to maintain consensus at the movement level. Upon their return to the Sebastia camp with a written and signed compromise, leaders of the movement learned that none other than Rabbi Kook rejected it. It is revealing that Rabbi Levinger, one of the most ardent key figures of the movement, stated,

"Even my mentor and rabbi Zvi Yehuda Kook needs to understand that it is the decision of the people on the ground that we need to accept and follow" (Huberman 2008: 110).

A final important point relates to how the coevolution and mutual reinforcement of the three relational mechanisms mitigated the influence of flanking and polarization. Palestinian attacks on settlers rose during 1975–1976, responding partly to the settlement drive (Tamari 1981). Additionally, differences in ideologies and worldviews between movement actors regarding, most centrally, attitudes toward progressive institutional actors, state authority, and the rule of law were in no short supply. Nevertheless, notwithstanding a handful of violent attacks on Palestinian property in Hebron during 1974 and occasional expressions of fundamentalist worldviews, the general pattern of contention that gradually took shape during the Sebastia campaign was predominantly nonviolent and unanimously pragmatic and integrationist (i.e., *Mamlakhti*).

4.1.2 Honeymoon Goes Aground

The period between the first and second Rabin governments (1974–1977; 1992–1995) and their respective protest campaigns – Sebastia and the Oslo Accords – saw two noteworthy opposing developments in the evolution of opportunity spirals. The first development related to the continued strengthening of the movement's strategic bargaining position following the Sebastia compromise in terms of activation of connections and brokerage. What started as a drizzle turned into a downpour of sympathetic ears of politicians, appointees, and public officials in almost every institution and agency relevant to the settlement enterprise following the victory of the Begin-led Likud in the 1977 general elections (Pedahzur 2012; Allegra and Maggor 2022). To a certain degree, many leading figures of the movement became *krovim la'malkhut* (i.e., cronies), with the doors of many cabinet members' offices, including the prime minister's, regularly open to them (Zertal and Eldar 2004). The solidification of this support network took place in late 1978, following the formation of a settlement body called *Amana* (Covenant) that enjoyed the formal backing and support of the state and then, shortly after, the formation of the YESHA Council (see Section 1) (Hirsch-Hoefler and Mudde 2020). In no time, this support network, called the YESHA lobby, became the most influential lobby inside Israel's corridors of power (Sprinzak 1991). So powerful was it that when Israel's Supreme Court of Justice began in 1979 to intervene in cases of land confiscations, determining some were unconstitutional for resting on political rather than security grounds, the movement and legal advisors for government ministries found creative solutions for the "land crisis" (Lustick 1981; Harnoy 1994).

Not all solutions led to new settlements – some resulted in the further development of existing ones, disappointing many movement actors. Moreover, some setbacks resulted from government decisions, as was the case, for example, with the freeze on new settlements and territorial withdrawals entailed in the Camp David Accords. These setbacks enraged the movement leadership because they represented the opposite direction to Begin's promise for many more settlements in the land of liberated Israel made just before he took office (Aronson 2008). But more than the disturbing realization that Begin's vision of the Greater Land of Israel was based on his idea of the historical right of the Jewish people, not on a divine right (Taub 2007), was the agonizing recognition of how narrow the movement's "wiggle room" became.

The Movement leadership contributed to this unfavorable evolution of opportunity spirals. In the wake of the Sebastia compromise, its cross-sectoral alliances had improved. For example, in early 1976, most Knesset members thwarted a government initiative to evict the settlers from Kaddum, a military base to which they had been relocated as part of the compromise. That majority rested on a broader, organized opposition from within Alignment's party base, which took the form of the Greater Land of Israel Loyalist Circle of the Labor Movement (also known as the Ein Vered Circle) (Shiloah 1989; Weisburd 1989; Peleg 2002). But then things changed substantially due to the dominant viewpoint within the Bloc secretariate to align with Likud before the 1977 elections. The belief on the part of many members of the Bloc secretariate that a political turnover to Likud would fundamentally change the situation in favor of the settlement mission proved to be shortsighted and politically unwise. Narrowing the movement's maneuvering space thus meant that it would be overly dependent on Likud and that a majority achieved with the potential support of NRP would still lack the broad, national consensus-like features it had enjoyed before with the support of Alignment.[24] Additionally, turning their back on Alignment so decisively led to resentment and feelings of betrayal among Alignment politicians and members of the party's base, including movement activists and supporters.

Nowhere were the repercussions of the movement's strategic mistake more felt than during the progression of the Camp David peacemaking process. Despite intensive lobbying and orchestrated demonstrations

---

[24] An interview with Rabbi Yoel Ben-Nun, a leading figure of the Bloc, broadcasted on Israeli television in 1998. Go to: https://archive.kan.org.il/main/vod/rebirth/.

throughout the country, some of which turned violent, both Camp David accords received overwhelming support among members of the Knesset. Frustrated by decreasing political leverage, several leading figures decided to "go political" and form a political party, as happened in October 1979 with the formation of Tehiya (revival). However, the establishment of the party even further hampered the movement's ability to form cross-sectoral alliances. Tehiya would receive three seats in the 1981 Knesset, sufficient to make some difference, yet at the expense of straining relations with the Likud and NRP even further.

The post-Yammit period and the second Likud-led government witnessed some improvement in the movement's bargaining position. Restoring ties and dialogue with Prime Minister Begin helped, and his successor in office in October 1983, Yitzhak Shamir, was an equally fervent believer in the Greater Israel vision. Between 1981 and 1984, the movement's supportive network ensured the approval of many new settlements and the expansion of many others. It nevertheless became clear that the narrower Likud-led coalition on which the movement had become overly dependent was consistently losing ground.

Despite its victory in the 1984 elections, Alignment failed to form a ruling coalition. Nevertheless, the party still managed to form a unity government with Likud, which was re-formed in late 1988 amidst an uncontrollable "first" Intifada. The political partnership between Likud and Alignment neutralized the movement's bargaining position and, as a result, consumed much of the remaining political leverage it could exert. It was not only that potential allies of the movement remained outside the ruling coalition (e.g., Tehiya with five seats) or were disqualified (e.g., *Kach*), but the influential positions of Alignment representatives enabled them to undermine and thwart the settlement enterprise directly (e.g., preventing allocation of funds to approved settlements) and indirectly (e.g., promoting peace initiatives and policies). A relative improvement in the strategic position of the movement took place following the formation of a rightwing government in June 1990 and the active settlement policy it tried to promote. However, this improvement was both too little and too brief. Prime Minister Shamir eventually capitulated to international pressure to consider the idea of Palestinian self-rule, which outraged movement actors and the broader rightwing camp. It prompted the withdrawal of several rightwing partners from the ruling coalition and the further fragmentation of the rightwing camp. These developments expedited the collapse of the government and paved the way for Alignment's (renamed Labor from then on) victory in the June 1992 elections.

4.1.3 Unwanted Children[25]

In and of itself, Labor's victory in the June 1992 elections, based on a commitment to advance the peace process with the Palestinians, did not drive radicalization forward. Prime Minister Rabin represented the "right flank" within his government, a point well noted by movement leaders and which acted as the basis for negotiations before and shortly after elections (Huberman 2008). Although a round of changing-of-the-guards followed the election, with many pro-settlement politicians clearing their offices and public officials fired, others remained, and still others were found among those just instituted (Pedahzur 2012). Finally, while the ruling coalition was predominantly leftwing on foreign and security issues, Rabin made earnest attempts to include rightwing and religious partners. Eventually, he succeeded in securing the inclusion of the ultra-Orthodox party *Shas*. Nevertheless, in a little over a year, the movement experienced one of the most meaningful challenges to its settlement agenda – the Oslo Accords – and experienced two of the most dreadful manifestations of radicalization.

Signs of the movement's noticeably diminishing bargaining position soon surfaced. In January 1993, for example, the government decided to revoke the status of most of the Occupied Territories settlements as development areas, which meant considerable cuts in financial benefits (*Yediot*, January 10, 1993, p. 10; Huberman 2008). But it was in the period surrounding the signing of the Oslo Accords in Washington on September 13, 1993, that the exceptionally weak political leverage of the movement became evident.

The government succeeded in securing the majority of Knesset votes in support of the first Oslo Accord. This was so despite *Shas's* withdrawal from the coalition and the abstention of its members from the vote,[26] and thanks to the external support of Israeli-Arab parties acting as a "blocking majority". Rabin's minority coalition did reasonably well during the next few years, including making peace with Jordan, engaging in persistent peace talks with Syria, and passing the second Oslo Accord in September 1995. As much as connections and brokerage at the administrative levels remained, their numbers decreased overall, and those at the executive and government levels drastically shrank. Moreover,

> Others, who did not work for the state but previously enjoyed unlimited access to those ministers [in charge of the formation of, and allocation of resources to settlements], were suddenly required to schedule appointments, which in most cases were repeatedly deferred … [R]abin himself avoided holding personal meetings with the settlers as much as he could. (Pedahzur 2012: 106)

---

[25] I borrow the term from della Porta and Tarrow's 1986 article "Unwanted Children" Political Violence and the Cycle of Protest in Italy, 1966–1973.

[26] *Shas* left the coalition several days before the vote following two Supreme Court rulings against two members indicted for bribery and fraud.

Box 3 Key dates and actors: Oslo Accords

July 13, 1992	Prime Minister Rabin forms a ruling coalition
December 16	End of bilateral Israeli-Arab peace talks in Washington
April 27, 1993	Resumption of peace talks in Washington between Israel and Palestinian representatives
August 29	Publication of a peace agreement signed in Oslo between Israel and PLO; treaty signed on September 13
September 14	*Shas* Party withdraws from the ruling coalition; Israel-Arab parties lend external support to the minority government
Mid-September	YESHA Council tries to lead the campaign and forms the "Joint Headquarter" as a special operational body
October 30	Onset of the "Jewish Intifada"
February 25, 1994	Massacre at the Cave of the Patriarchs
March 13	The Government declares *Kach* and Kahane Chai as terrorist organizations and outlaws both
April 6	Hamas and Islamic Jihad's suicide terrorism campaign begins
May 3	Halakhic ruling prohibiting soldiers' participation in evacuation of Jewish settlements
May 4	Establishment of the Palestinian Authority and a civil police force
October 26	Peace treaty signed between Israel and Jordan
May 34, 1995	A US-brokered negotiation between Syria and Israel yields an agreement regarding security in the Golan Heights.
September 28	Signing the second Oslo Accord
November 4, 1995	Assassination of Prime Minister Rabin during a peace rally in Tel Aviv

4.2 Opportunity Spirals under Threat and Radicalization

The ramifications of the Oslo Accords for the settlement enterprise and its population were so far-reaching (e.g., Palestinian self-government with ruling powers, withdrawal from areas in the Territories, release of Palestinian prisoners) that the exceptionally weak political leverage of the movement became conspicuous. An indication of this is offered in Figure 7, showing the dramatic increase in the level of contention following the exposure of the secret talks and the agreement reached in Oslo in late August 1993. While disruptive events seem to predominate throughout, the relative portion of violent events (denoted in data labels) tends to exceed that of conventional events. This contrasts with the relatively mild and short response to the resumption of peace talks between Israelis and Palestinians (announced in late April 1993), which was less disruptive and violent overall.

Figure 7 does not show the composition of movement actors initiating or involved in contention and the objects of their actions. Of the total number of contentious events during this period ($n = 363$), some were the initiative of ultra-radical organizations whose actions were entirely dictated by extremist world-views and who acted independently from the other, more pragmatic movement actors. Other events were the initiatives of newly formed, mostly radical and militant organizations (e.g., *Mate Ma'amatz* [Effort Center], *Zu Artzenu* [This is Our Land]). These organizations were willing to cooperate with the YESHA Council as long as it served their interests and gradually gained momentum at the latter's expense.

The diversity of forces reflected the mounting difficulties the Council faced trying to lead the campaign and mobilize consensus. One problem was that the Council did not try to coordinate activities with all organizations and groups, particularly the ultra-radical, who were seen as responsible for the downfall of Shamir's government and were pushed aside when they tried to join protest activities. Another problem was that the Council lacked experience in organizing effective street struggles. After organizing an impressive demonstration against the Accords in early September and then seemingly losing impetus by deciding to continue with only a costly public relations campaign, it was criticized for letting its semi-institutional position dictate its restrained action strategy (Sprinzak 1999). When several of its members drafted a plan for the preservation of "settlement blocs" (i.e., densely concentrated settlement areas) and proposed it to Prime Minister Rabin in early November, they were criticized vehemently by other movement actors for daring to accept the Accords *de facto*. They were also criticized by other Council members, who suspended their membership (Huberman 2008: 261; *Yediot*, November 10, 1993).

The Council became one of many organizations in a campaign that gradually turned violent and, to an extent, indiscriminately so. While many contentious events targeted Palestinians, a considerable portion involved other objects of claims and of attacks. In addition to sporadic instances of violence directed at Israeli progressive activists and journalists, there was mounting evidence of

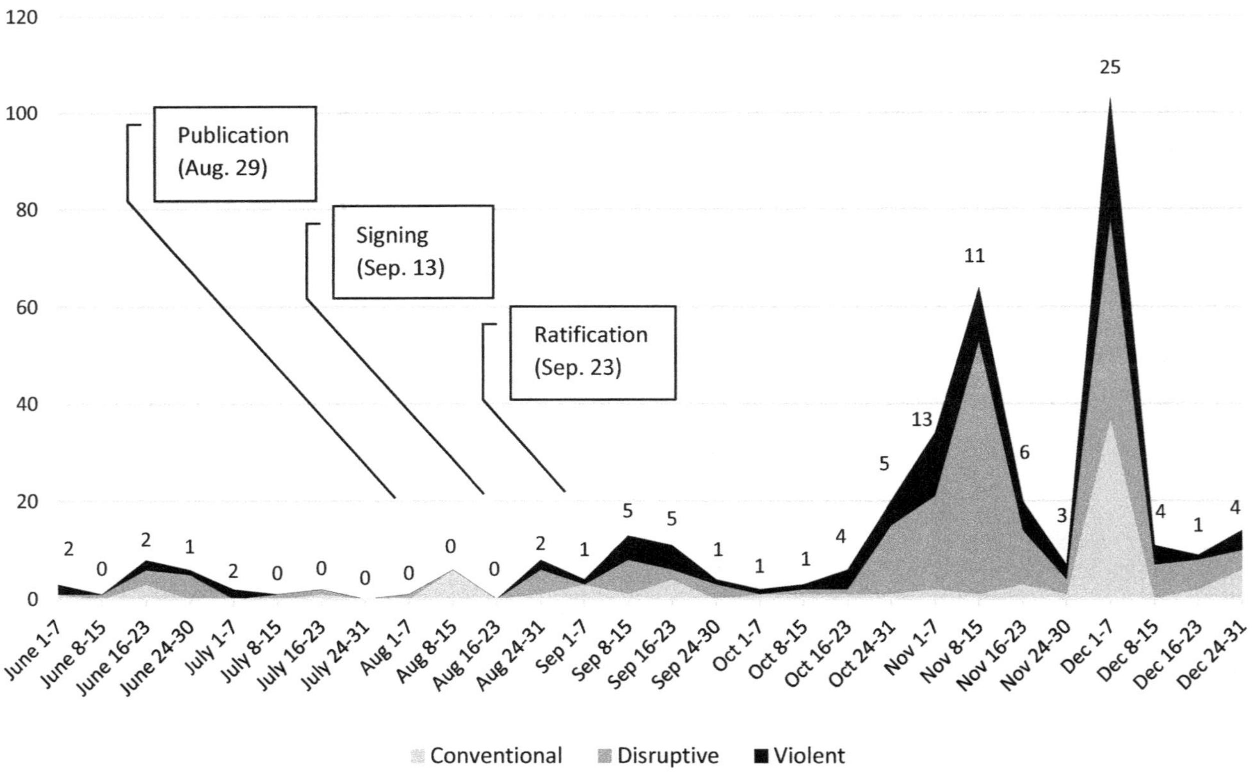

Figure 7 Movement Contention Surrounding the Oslo Accords

willingness on the part of movement activists to engage in violent confrontations with the police and, critically, attacks against IDF property and forces. Ultra-radical organizations acted early on, like *Kach* and a splinter faction called *Kahane Chai* (Hebrew for Kahane lives). They formed armed militias that were trained in the US and made it clear that this time they would not follow the Yammit model of collective suicide, but would rather raise arms and "shoot to kill any soldier trying to evict us" (*Yediot*, June 10, 1993, p. 11). On September 23, 1993, the day of Knesset ratification of the first Oslo Accord, IDF forces were sent to evict hundreds of settlers from two newly erected settlements (later called "outposts") near the West Bank Palestinian cities of Hebron and Ramallah. The operations involved no attempt to engage in dialogue and consultation and quickly turned violent.

In the context of exceptionally weak political leverage, the salience of flanking and polarization increased, consequently propelling radicalization. Instances of Palestinian attacks began stirring up retaliatory, vengeful attacks in far greater frequency, intensity, and scope. A ruthless murder of a resident of a West Bank settlement on October 30, 1993, prompted a wave of unruly and violent contention against Palestinians throughout the Occupied Territories, involving a growing number of movement activists. This "Jewish Intifada" lasted for months, responsive to Palestinian counter-attacks and reactions of the Israeli political and security authorities. One such response was a government plan, initially raised and discussed in the Knesset plenum on November 23, 1993, regarding how to improve the effectiveness of law enforcement on Jewish settlers in the Occupied Territories. The proposed government plan turned out to be prophetic. In the early morning hours of February 25, 1994, when hundreds of Palestinian worshippers prayed in the Cave of the Patriarchs' Hall of Isaac in Hebron, Baruch Goldstein, a settler and *Kach* activist, approached them quietly while they were in supplication on their knees. He tossed a hand grenade into the center of the room and immediately opened fire on them. By the time his weapon jammed and several worshippers neutralized him, he had killed 29 and injured 125 people (Pedahzur and Perliger 2009).

Movement actors justified the violence that characterized the Jewish Intifada in ways that portrayed Jewish settlers and, more broadly, Israeli-Jewish citizens, as victims of a government without legal or moral grounds. That government, so it was argued, rendered the blood of its loyal citizens permissible by relentlessly moving forward with a disastrous policy. This ideational system of justification was not new. Still, as the Oslo peace process progressed, it became more militant and zealous and began to appeal to hitherto more moderate and pragmatic movement activists. Indeed, even the relatively moderate YESHA Rabbinical Council began to adopt more militant views and ruled, in a communique to the settler population, that the shooting of Palestinian attackers and their collaborators was legitimate (Sprinzak 1999: 230–233). Prime Minister Rabin and members of his close circle responded in kind, beginning with statements like "I couldn't care less about them," continuing with "whiners" and "Kugelagers" (i.e., people who make a lot of noise and vent hot air), to making the analogy between Palestinian Hamas and settler militias (Sprinzak media collection: *Ma'ariv*, November 5, 1993).

Expressions of polarization reached new heights when the government outlawed *Kach* and Kahane Chai shortly following the atrocity in the Cave of the Patriarchs, and began to seriously consider evacuating settlers from Hebron. It was also when control over most of the Gaza Strip and the Jericho vicinity in the West Bank was handed to the newly-formed Palestinian Authority, and the wave of suicide attacks initiated by Hamas and the Islamic Jihad in Israeli cities began in full force. Three authoritative rabbis in Israel's Religious-Zionist milieu issued a *halakhic* ruling prohibiting soldiers from participating in the evacuation of Jewish settlements in the Greater Land of Israel. According to the ruling, "not only was the government committing a heinous crime against God and Jewish history, but it was ready to do so with the help of Arabs" (Sprinzak 1999: 250). Despite a public uproar and calls for restraints and moderation by many public figures, rightwing politicians and moderate rabbis included, polarization deepened even further. When the government moved forward with the peace process despite the worsening Palestinian suicide attacks, Prime Minister Rabin was depicted as Adolf Hitler and, together with Foreign Minister Peres, were referred to as the worst kinds of Jews whose killing is justified, even warranted, according to Jewish *Halakha* (Sprinzak 1999).

In this context of unprecedented polarization and increasingly harsh militancy, activists became more violent. In late 1993, an underground group was formed by two ultra-radical rightwing activists, Yigal Amir and his brother Hagai, for the purpose of halting the peace process. According to Pedahzur and Perliger (2009, Ch. 5), who studied the case most comprehensively and systematically, the brothers and a gradually broadening, albeit small network of like-minded activists considered and even test-ran several schemes and acted (most likely successfully) to secure rabbinical authorization for the killing. The plan that was eventually carried out was to look for an opportunity to enable one of them to penetrate the security cordon surrounding Rabin and shoot him from close range. The opportunity presented itself toward the end of an impressive mass rally in support of the peace process in Tel Aviv on November 4, 1995. Armed with a Beretta, Yigal Amir quietly approached Rabin and his security cordon as they were heading to the prime minister's car and shot him dead from close range.

The assassination of Prime Minister Rabin did not stop the Oslo peace process. Nor did the return to power of Likud (headed by Benyamin Netanyahu) in the 1996 general elections dramatically improve the movement's strategic bargaining position and political leverage. Despite improvement in the pool of brokers and connections at the political and administrative levels, high-level politicians and public officials with no settlement agenda were in office, including the minister of defense and his aide for settlement affairs. Moreover, the predominantly rightwing ruling coalition and the absence of any meaningful opposition parties willing to consider an alliance with the movement in the post-Rabin assassination period meant that the movement was highly dependent on the government.[27] Prime Minister Netanyahu's demonstrated commitment to working with the Clinton Administration and moving forward with the Oslo Accords – for example, a decision to maintain strict limitations on the construction of new settlements – prompted two developments. First, increasingly deepening disagreements between ruling coalition members culminated in several coalition partners' withdrawal and brought about Netanyahu's downfall in late December 1998. The second concerned deepening rifts and factionalism at the movement level following indications of pragmatism on the part of the YESHA Council (e.g., working with the government to make adjustments to the maps of pending territorial withdrawals) (Huberman 2008). Small groups of primarily young activists broke ranks and moved to establish outposts outside the major settlement blocs and, eventually, to cultivate an oppositional subculture. As discussed in the concluding section, this "Hilltop Youth" network played a central role in the radicalization that developed in the post-Gaza Pullout campaign.

The landslide victory of Labor, led by Ehud Barak, in the May 1999 elections and the unprecedented broad coalition he managed to form (75 out of 120 seats) played into the hands of the movement. The coalition included several important rightwing parties and factions, providing ample brokers and allies to the movement. Moreover, the large number of coalition partners made it easier to form alliances, facilitating the formation of an "opposition within the coalition" over several settlement-related issues. Complementing the potentially enabling political conditions was the decision of the YESHA Council to try to work with the government, which led to understandings between the sides regarding blueprints for the government settlement policy. The problem was that Prime Minister Barak was committed to progressing with the Oslo Accords and had

---

[27] Though Labor received the majority of the votes in the elections, Netanyahu formed the government following implementation of direct elections for prime minister in 1996, given the tight majority of popular votes he received over those of Peres. Israel would return (with several amendments) to the previous parliamentary electoral system in 2003.

more than enough coalition partners to bolster that commitment. However, the minute Barak began to move forward with additional territorial withdrawals and the evacuation of illegal outposts, his ruling coalition began disintegrating, leading to new elections for prime minister in March 2001.

Finally, Ariel Sharon's victory in the March 2001 elections held many promises for the movement's agenda and goals. Not only was the bloody and ferocious Al-Aqsa Intifada raging, which made the peace process seem not only unfeasible but also undesirable, but Sharon was, on balance, one of the oldest supporters and most influential brokers of the settlement enterprise. When the elections to the Knesset took place in January 2003, and the Sharon-led Likud doubled its size in the Knesset and formed a predominantly rightwing coalition, these promises seemed even more bright. However, it was none other than Prime Minister Sharon who introduced the idea of a "disengagement plan" in late 2003.

4.3 Opportunity Spirals during the Gaza Pullout

In light of the unprecedented gravity and scope of the Gaza Pullout Plan, intensifying Palestinian attacks, and the unfortunately rich history of radicalization on the part of movement actors, both the movement and the government recognized the high potential for violence and their mutual interest in curbing it. Despite their conflicting goals, they converged on the importance of matching their expectations and understandings regarding the boundaries of legitimate struggle and rules of engagement. This was facilitated by the involvement of many individual actors from both sides in the emergence and evolution of the relational practices and routines that had constituted opportunity spirals during past campaigns, and the appreciation of their role in containing radicalization. It was clear to both that more than the eventual shape of government policy, the strength of the movement's bargaining position and ability to exercise political leverage would make the difference in terms of preventing violent resistance and aggression.

Indeed, throughout the campaign, efforts were made by both sides to refrain from engaging in mutually delegitimizing and vilifying language and to try to forge a clear separation between the Israeli and the Palestinian fronts. On the part of the prime minister and the government, this meant continuous efforts to coordinate the impending evacuation from Gaza with the Palestinian Authority via various channels, based on the condition that "there will be no disengagement under fire" (Haloutz 2010: 316). Prime Minister Sharon and heads of the IDF were fully aware of the possibility that Palestinian attacks would deepen frustration and indignation among the settlement population and play into the hands of the ultra-radical organizations (Ibid.). There was also a conscious decision made early on to avoid antagonizing and sweeping derogatory language, no matter how heated the struggle would become in rhetoric and deeds. According to the chief strategic and media advisor of the prime minister's office, it was clear from the outset of the need to "insist in rhetoric and deeds that Sharon was the prime minister of everybody, including theirs, and to never use negative antagonizing terminology . . . They are not the enemies of peace . . . We should not delegitimize them as a whole, only those that use or call for engagement in violence."

On the part of the movement leadership, an explicit link was made between the conception of *Mamlakhtiyut* (i.e., integrationist – being an integral part of state and society) and the political standing it afforded, on the one hand, and the importance of containing the ultra-radical elements within the movement, on the other. For GKAC leaders, as discussed in Section 1, Palestinian attacks had the unintended positive consequence of bringing a tide of newcomers to the settlements, which benefited their agenda of connecting with the Israeli public. For the Council, it was directly and significantly political. As noted in Section 1, it was about staying relevant, realizing that violent reactions would seriously hamper their traditional agenda of *Mamlakhtiyut*, and hence their institutional and public standing. According to one of the heads of the Council, "We agreed on the overall strategy according to which those who claim to represent and lead the Israeli society cannot revert to violence as this would be self-defeating, disconnecting us from society at large."

It was not surprising then that efforts were made at the movement level and between the movement and the IDF to prevent ultra-radical activists from infiltrating the Gush Katif region. When infiltration did occur, both sides worked together to take control of the situation – as discussed in Section 2. Furthermore, despite the harsh criticism of Prime Minister Sharon and his plan for unilateral territorial withdrawal, leaders of the movement tried to avoid sweeping derogatory rhetoric. Gush Katif Action Committee and, even more, the Council, demonstrated a sophisticated understanding of the political circumstances and the complexities of the political process.

Admittedly, however, the ability of Prime Minister Sharon and his allies to make progress with the Plan made the ability of the movement leadership to preserve the dominance of *Mamlakhtiyut* particularly difficult, even among those traditionally considered moderate. When it became clear that Sharon refused to accept the results of the Likud referendum of early May 2004, he began to be portrayed among radical and ultra-radical circles as a ruthless dictator, irrecoverably corrupted, and as someone who engaged in dirty and petty politics. On October 1, 2004, several weeks before the Knesset's first reading of the "Disengagement Bill," none other than an editorial in the moderate *Ha'Tzofe* daily newspaper presented Sharon as responsible for the transfer of Jews and their death at the hands of Palestinian assailants.

Nevertheless, movement actors were deeply convinced that it was possible to abolish the Plan. Figure 8 is based on content analysis of print media items from four movement news outlets: *Ad-Kan, Ha'Tzofe, Nekuda,* and *B'Sheva*. It presents the distribution of "integrationist talk" (i.e., the *Mamlakhti* approach) regarding multiple state institutions and how it varied in relation to "perception of efficacy" following several critical events.[28] The most important finding relates to how levels of perception of efficacy remained relatively high and positive even when levels of integrationist talk dropped and became more segregationist (i.e., the *anti-Mamlakhti* approach) in their valence. The drop was most marked following both the Referendum Act and the imposition of the Blockade and included the Knesset and the military – two of Israel's most valued state institutions.

The best way to make sense of the findings is by considering the strong bargaining position of the movement and the impressive political leverage

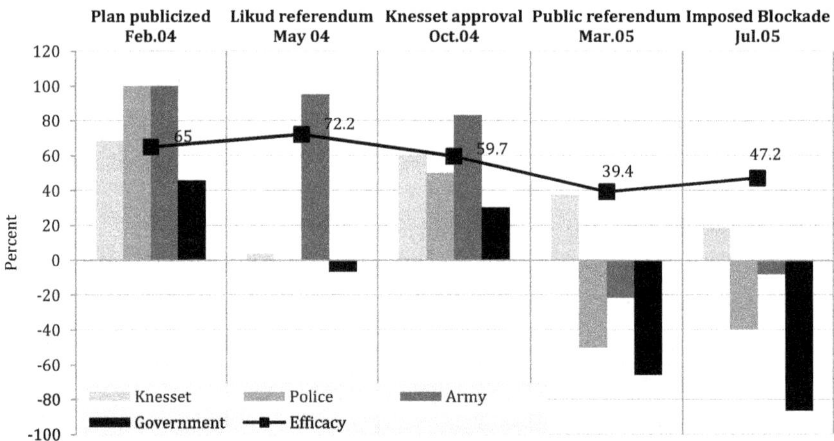

Figure 8 Specific integrationist talk and efficacy by events

• Integrationist score for "prime minister" is constantly negative and above −50

• Integrationist score for "legal system" is negative and above −20 (except for Plan Publicized, where the score is 16.6)

Source: Alimi, Eitan Y. 2018. "Struggling to Remain Relevant": Why and How Radicalization Was Impeded in the Struggle against the Gaza Pullout." *Canadian Review of Sociology,* 55(4): 597–623.

---

[28] The calculation of scores is based on the same logic as in Figure 1-a (Section 1).

its leaders managed to exercise. The list of political achievements the movement leadership was involved or central in obtaining is astonishing. Particularly noteworthy were (1) the victory of anti-Pullout party center members in the Likud internal referendum; (2) withdrawal from the ruling coalition of entire party factions; (3) bringing the Knesset to vote on a Public Referendum bill for the first time in the history of the state; (4) bringing the Knesset and relevant committees to make numerous adjustments to the "evacuation-compensation law" that generously expanded the criteria for eligibility and calculation of the compensation rate; and (5) playing a pivotal role in initiating the vote of no-confidence in the government of May 30, 2005, which failed by a thread.

This impressive record of political achievements corresponded to the exceptional effectiveness of the combined use of the three relational practices and routines. The pool of connections the movement managed to activate over the years to support its goals broadened and tightened. An impressive number of allies existed among members of the Knesset, ministers, deputy ministers, the prime minister's office, party institutions, and within-party movements, as well as among public officials at various levels, including CEOs of governmental ministries. Public and media figures and other influencers supported the movement (Hirsch-Hoefler and Mudde 2020). Those belonging to the latter made sure to express their sympathy with the struggle in public appearances and statements; others joined demonstrations, vigils, rallies, and other types of public displays, even composing songs in support of the struggle; still others paid visits of sympathy to the Gush Katif settlements, and some went so far as to relocate their residences there. Finally, and critically, it was the insistence of Prime Minister Sharon, handed down clearly and explicitly to members of his close circle and the cabinet to adopt an open-door policy vis-à-vis leaders of the movement. According to a senior official at the Prime Minister's Office, lessons learned from the struggle against the Yammit evacuation were strictly followed, particularly vis-à-vis the disconnect between Prime Minister Begin and leaders of the opposition groups. "It was made clear to all to always maintain contact and dialogue with them, whether secretively or openly, and no matter how intense and offensive their opposition become." The words of one of the leaders of GKAC corroborate this: "There was an ongoing, continuous dialogue with many ministers while other politicians tried to reach out to us. I cannot say that doors were closed to us."

Some of those contacts also acted as brokers from Likud and other rightwing coalition partners. These brokers played a crucial role in several related manners: Some maintained contact and kept communication channels open between movement representatives and representatives of the prime minister's office and coalition partners, which became particularly important when tensions skyrocketed surrounding key developments. Such was the case regarding government approval of the Plan in early June 2004. Despite brokering efforts by several Likud members to preserve the coalition while securing the movement's goals, Sharon's success in securing a majority within the government resulted in the withdrawal of a rightwing coalition partner, the National Union. It also caused a rift within another rightwing coalition partner, NRP, over whether or not to follow in the National Union's footsteps. Other brokers alleviated tension and managed coordination between movement actors, particularly between the pragmatic and the ultra-radical elements. Their involvement in many contentious events strengthened their standing as reliable brokers and gave them a much-needed comprehension of intra-movement relational dynamics, which was particularly useful after the fall of the Public Referendum bill of March 2005 and the shifting gravity of the struggle to the streets. Finally, there were those who made sure to secure, and at times tighten, coordination between the movement and the IDF and police. This became particularly critical following the incident of a settler using his personal military weapon to resist the eviction of an illegal outpost in January 2005, which brought all sides to agree that both evacuators and evacuees should be unarmed.

Finally, alongside the impressive and effective pool of ties and the diversity of brokers, possibilities for forming alliances were equally rich and meaningful. These possibilities included partners outside the ruling coalition, as was the case with the ultra-orthodox party *Shas*, whose members repeatedly voted against the government Pullout Plan. There were also partners inside the ruling coalition, as with both NRP and National Union, who worked closely with the movement and were responsible for some of the most meaningful achievements throughout the campaign. However, allying with forces within the Likud proved to be critical.

True, the Sharon-led Likud won nearly forty seats in the 2003 elections and could form a broad ruling coalition relatively quickly without too many partners. But what Sharon did not anticipate was the fierce and organized opposition he would face from within the Likud. This organized opposition, the "Likud Rebels," included thirteen highly respected members of the Knesset who promised they would make the life of Prime Minister Sharon miserable. They did this in cooperation with other members of the Knesset under the driving force and coordinating efforts of the YESHA Council. To add to the above list of achievements, in late 2004, Sharon was heading a minority government and was forced to invite the ultra-orthodox parties and then Labor to join the ruling coalition. In the Knesset vote on the approval of the new government on January 10, 2005, the "rebels" lost by only two votes.

Expectedly, the failure to obtain the critical parliamentary mass necessary for "averting the evil decree" was associated with increasingly dissenting and polarizing voices calling for social and political segregation. These voices also accused the government of handing victory to Palestinian terrorism and pointed to the continuing, at times intensifying, rocket fire and other attacks as proof of such folly. Nevertheless, these voices' separate and joint influences were mitigated by the continuing, undeniably impressive assurances of political leverage the central leadership of the movement provided. Together with the ability of the leadership to manage consensus mobilization at the intra-movement level and to maintain underbidding with the security forces, it became possible to put a brake on radicalization.

5 Lessons from the Gaza Pullout

This Element's analysis of relation-building within the Settlement Movement and between it and the Israeli state and its agents of social control invites us to think differently about the movement than do analyses that center on cognitive or environmental forces. The focus on how relations within and between the various contending parties emerged and evolved over time and across contexts gives rise to a more nuanced understanding of the movement's history of activism. Indeed, while there is a rich historical record of radicalization by movement actors, that history also witnessed instances of contained radicalization, sometimes against all odds.

The contribution of a relational mode of investigation to a more nuanced and balanced understanding of a movement that is infamous for its rich history of radicalization is not limited to the Israeli case. Other movements come to mind, with the Protestant Unionist Movement that developed during the "Troubles" in Northern Ireland bearing more than a passing resemblance. While there are unquestionably differences in social boundaries, regime type, and other initial conditions, it is possible to point to similar relational dynamics that were successful in containing radicalization in the struggle against the Anglo-Irish Agreement of November 1985. The campaign against the signing of the Agreement, representing one of several attempts to promote a political settlement to the conflict, began several months earlier in June, after it became known publicly. The fact that movement actors, including institutional ones (e.g., the Ulster Unionist Party), were not informed of and excluded from the negotiations and talks was a cause of great concern among the Protestant-Unionist community. With a history of fragmentation and unity resting only on the widespread suspicion that the pending Agreement would undermine their privileged status, such exclusion weakened the ability of the central and more pragmatic leadership to contain the ultra-radical groups. Despite efforts to establish consensus over strategy, tactics, and goals among the various movement groupings, paramilitary groups, such as the Ulster Defence Association, occasionally broke ranks and engaged in blatant violence. Nevertheless, the struggle against the signing of the Agreement saw relatively low levels of violence. The ability to prevent higher levels of violence related to the concentrated efforts by Unionist leaders to use their strong bargaining position to pressure Prime Minister Margaret Thatcher to consider meaningful changes to the draft agreement. It also related to these leaders' earnest attempts to work closely and coordinate their contentious activity with heads of the local security and police forces (Cochrane 1997; Elliott and Flackes 1999).

Apart from presenting an additional exemplary case of contained radicalization, what takeaways can we glean from the preceding analysis of forestalled violent resistance, and how do they help us make sense of more recent instances of settler radicalization? Specifically, though not exclusively, I am referring to the grassroots network known as *Noar Ha'Gevaot* (Hilltop Youth) and the violent action strategy most closely associated with it, called *Tag Mekhir* (Price Tag), which acquired voice at the heels of the Gaza Pullout and has been gaining traction ever since. In contrast to other strategies of contention, such as bargaining, persuasion, or even vigilantism, the Price Tag strategy privileges coercion and deterrence, and threatens to take a heavy toll on anyone opposing or acting against the settlement enterprise.

The first takeaway is that *to be effective, efforts to contain radicalization should not focus primarily on cognitive and environmental forces*. The idea that it is not enough to cope with militancy or motives and propensities for aggression by relying chiefly on cognitive and environmental measures echoes Tilly's (2003) general point that for "relation people" the way to restrain violence is by restoring relations. Tilly did not pursue this line of investigation, but he did point in its direction. As we saw, neither attempts to prevent further polarization through conciliatory rhetoric nor coping with flanking through improvement in the material conditions of the settlement population proved sufficient for restraining settler violence. Efforts at containing radicalization usually involve groups with a history of radicalization, whose members are socially withdrawn and whose behavior is heavily shaped by ideologies and environmental stimuli. It is therefore essential to proactively engage ultra-radical actors in order to contain them.

Regarding attempts to minimize polarization, such was the case with the disapproval and call for restraint expressed by moderate movement spiritual leaders in response to the rabbinical ruling calling for soldier disobedience in the context of the struggle against the Oslo Accords. These efforts, as we know, did little in the way of containing the ultra-radicals through actual engagement. That lesson had been strictly followed during the Gaza Pullout campaign when leaders from all contending parties bolstered their decision to avoid derogatory language with relational practices and routines, a decision that ultimately proved effective. The analysis of the Gaza Pullout campaign also demonstrates the futility of mainly focusing on material conditions to contain radicalization. True, high governmental and IDF officials tried to coordinate the Pullout with the Palestinian Authority in order to stop Palestinian attacks, but this should not lead us to gloss over the relation work conducted in earnest with movement actors, which proved effective in minimizing settler violence even when instances of Palestinian attacks increased. Supportive evidence began to pile up as early as the first Intifada, when contentious interaction between settlers and Palestinian activists reached unprecedented levels, and yet were driven by different logics. The moderating effect of the approach of Major-General Mitzna, the Central Command commander, on levels and forms of settler contention when the Intifada was raging is one more case in point.

Contradicting evidence of predominant reliance on cognitive and environmental forces helps make sense of post-Pullout instances of settler radicalization. The Pullout did not bring an end to international pressure for more territorial withdrawals or to the Israeli government's willingness to consider compromises along similar lines. In addition to more resolute efforts by Israeli governments to establish some measure of control over the broadening phenomenon of illegal outposts were signs of greater willingness to consider additional pullouts.

Contentious interactions during late December 2005 and early 2006 made it clear that the Pullout indeed sharpened militancy among certain movement actors who called for violent resistance to attempts to evict outposts as a redemptive act meant to "erase the disgrace of Gush Katif" (Roth 2014). These ultra-radical forces also initiated violent attacks on Palestinians more frequently than before. Even though the level of Palestinian rocket fire was considerably lower compared to the pre-Pullout period, they argued that calls made by politicians and IDF officers before the Pullout saying that the Pullout would bolster Palestinian terrorism (Ben-Eliezer 2012) proved correct.

Nevertheless, it also became clear that the Pullout did not eliminate moderate and pragmatic voices who warned against extremism and called for lawful behavior and the importance of maintaining an integrationist approach (i.e., *Mamlakhtiyut*). Importantly, this latter stance, shared by representatives within the political system and among senior IDF and police officers, did not translate into relation work in any meaningful way. The First Rain military operation of late September 2005, meant to completely stop rocket fire from the Gaza Strip, saw no lessening of settler violence against both Palestinian and IDF targets in the West Bank. What characterized the series of struggles against eviction of illegal West Bank outposts this time related to the lack of serious coordinating efforts between the various contending parties and within them. It also related to decisions made by the IDF to let a joint force of police, border guard police, and riot police be in charge of carrying out evictions, and to minimize direct contact with evicted settlers as much as possible. The absence of meaningful relation work was accompanied by a developing "war mentality" on the part of Sharon's successor in office, Ehud Olmert, and leaders of what became a coalition of ultra-radical groups, including Hilltop Youth activists, resulted in several rounds of escalating violence.

The brute violence that characterized the struggles of late December 2005 and early 2006 turned out to be a prelude to the dramatic progression of radicalization during Prime Minister Olmert's term, primarily surrounding the Annapolis Middle East peace conference of late November 2007. The peace talks between Israeli and Palestinian delegates discussing, among other topics, additional pullouts, brought about heightening tension between contending parties on the Israeli side. By that time, however, the Hilltop Youth phenomenon had gained strength in social and financial terms and, along with other group members of the ultra-radical coalition, presented a meaningful internal opposition to the YEHSA Council. Socially, this coalition developed various networks of support, including religious figures offering symbolic certification. Financially, it benefited from newly formed voluntary associations that were budgeted by state-funded local and regional municipalities.

Similar to the immediate post-Pullout period, there were no meaningful or systematic efforts at relation-building, but mainly efforts to tamp down militancy with calls for moderation following intensifying calls for violence. Additional efforts centered on restraining propensities for aggression in light of the dramatic increase in Hamas-led attacks and rocket fire from the Gaza Strip. As the sole power controlling the Gaza Strip,[29] Hamas tried to undermine the peace talks in opposition to both Israel and the West Bank-based Palestinian Authority. Seen from this perspective, it is no wonder that the struggles against the eviction of illegal outposts that followed Annapolis saw such high levels of violence exercised by both sides, and no coincidence that the first Price Tag incident took place in August 2008.

The second takeaway is that *relational mechanisms operate in mutually reinforcing and variable ways in putting a brake on radicalization.* This takeaway builds on a point well substantiated by scholars of radicalization who

---

[29] Hamas took power following the January 2006 elections to the Palestinian Legislative Council. In June 2007, Hamas took over the Strip after five days of bloody clashes with Fatah-led Palestinian Authority officials.

follow a relational persuasion: It takes two to radicalize. The ability to put a brake on engagement in violence, it is argued, grows out of relations between at least two and usually more actors; hence, the more relations restored the better (e.g., Goodwin 2007; Alimi et al. 2015). Less stressed and substantiated is the point that the ability to put a brake on radicalization rests less on a mixture of relational forces with additive effects than on the way they combine to form, in the aggregate, a compounded effect. Our analytical history of relation-building helps reveal not only how relational mechanisms get in the way of one another and undermine efforts at containing radicalization, but also how mechanisms support each other's operation in dynamic and variable ways and aggregately strengthen efforts at containing radicalization. As discussed, this mutual reinforcement is a function of the interdependence between mechanisms and their respective arenas of interaction, an interdependence that is the result of overlapping interacting actors and the cross-arena implications of the operation of each mechanism. As illustrated, expressions of mutual reinforcement began to appear as early as the Sebastia campaign of 1974–1975: Opportunity spirals supported (through brokerage and activation of connections) the ability to mobilize consensus (by demonstrating the competence of the movement leadership) and the development of underbidding (through rank matching and consultation between the movement leadership and heads of the IDF). This emerging pattern of mutual support among the mechanisms that prevented higher levels of settler violence. As also illustrated, the compounded effect of mutual reinforcement on containing radicalization reached full strength during the anti-Pullout campaign, though not necessarily through the same or similar configuration of practices and routines of the mechanisms.

It is possible to explain much of the enhanced radicalization of the coalition of ultra-radicals and the increased salience of the Price Tag strategy by a reversed pattern of mutual reinforcement, namely, a pattern of a mutually disintegrating operation of opportunity spirals, consensus mobilization, and underbidding. The process of complete disintegration of consensus mobilization among movement actors, which became evident most strongly following the Annapolis Peace Conference (2007), when ultra-radical forces formed an alternative to the YESHA Council, shaped (and was shaped by) similar processes of unfavorable opportunity spirals and collapsed underbidding. Regarding opportunity spirals, despite the victory of the Netanyahu-led Likud in the 2009 national elections and the consequent apparent regain of some of the Council's bargaining position, it soon became clear that Netanyahu capitalized on the disintegration process at the movement level and the resulting fragmentation of the movement's electoral potential into several political parties and factions. In addition to marginalizing ultra-radical forces within the Likud,

Netanyahu preferred to form a ruling coalition with Labor and the moderate, politically weak NRP (renamed *Bayit Yehudi* [Jewish Home]), rather than with its rival, the more radical and politically stronger religious-Zionist/Nationalist party, *Ha'Ikhud Ha'Leumi* (National Union).

Regarding underbidding, partly because of the headstrong position of Minister of Defense (and former Chief of General Staff) Ehud Barak, and partly the result of the (at times violent) disruption by ultra-radical forces of any understanding between senior IDF officers and the Council, the relationship between the sides reached critical heights of hostility. Amidst intense conflict between twenty-five rabbis, heads of *Yeshivot Hesder*, and the government over the former's support for disobedience and intensification of retaliatory attacks against Palestinians, we saw several rounds of blatant violence between ultra-radical forces and the police forces during the eviction of outposts (e.g., the September 2012 eviction of the West Bank outpost of Migron). These violent evictions were often followed by Price Tag violence against Palestinians and, crucially, IDF forces and property. Between 2011 and 2014, the number of Price Tag attacks reached its highest levels, at times with more than ten reported attacks per month (Eiran and Krause 2016). Expectedly, the hitherto most widespread and prolonged military operation in Gaza Strip, called the 2014 Gaza War or Operation Protective Edge, was taken advantage of by Hilltop Youth and other ultra-radical forces, settler and non-settler alike, to intensify Price Tag violence not only against Palestinians in the Occupied Territories but against Israeli-Arabs inside Israeli cities. It took a highly concentrated and orchestrated crackdown operation involving all Israeli security forces on Price Taggers during 2015 to bring about a significant (albeit temporary) decrease in such attacks.

Finally, the specific pattern of mutual reinforcement of relational mechanisms may shift as a result of changes in the immediate context of contentious politics or in the values and interests of one or more contending parties and actors. As a third and last takeaway, it seems that regardless of the specific pattern of mutual reinforcement, *certain ties and contacts between actors and parties score higher than others in containing radicalization*. The idea of meaningful ties directs attention to the role of specific relations in the larger network of contacts, whose relative weight is exceptionally high and cannot be fully gauged or assessed quantitatively. The qualitative strength of these ties may be the result of past experiences and lessons learned by contending actors or attributed to the central role and embedded position of one or more of the actors.

The possibility that a tie can be qualitatively meaningful yet quantitatively weak speaks again to the added value of a historically sensitive analysis of relation-building. A recurring finding from the analysis relates to the exceptionally meaningful relations between the movement and the IDF, as captured in the emergence and operation of underbidding. The qualitative strength of this set of ties and contacts was embedded in the symbiotic relationship that took shape most markedly following the June 1967 War and continued to consolidate subsequently in a variety of ways. Nowhere was this qualitative strength demonstrated more powerfully than in the struggle against the evacuation of Yammit, when the containment approach of IDF forces proved critical in preventing much higher levels of violence. But it was also the lesson learned by heads of both the security and political authorities regarding the centrality of the movement's spiritual leadership. While scoring fairly low on centrality measures (see Figure 5 in Section 2) the spiritual leadership was high in containing the ultra-radicals. On top of boosting the credence and legitimacy of the field leadership, the involvement of the spiritual leadership most emphatically embodied the synergic structure of relations between the movement and the IDF, to which they had contributed over the years.

The collapse of underbidding between the movement and the IDF, resulting, for example, in the resolute crackdown of security forces against ultra-radical Price Taggers and the break with more than twenty *Yeshivot Hesder* rabbis, expedited a meaningfully shift in the nature of relations between the two parties. In recent years, it is possible to identify a change from the traditionally mutually benefiting symbiotic relationship to one that is more competitive and, at times, even more conflict-heavy. In and of itself, the developing competitive symbiosis between the two parties is the result of the continuing increase in the number of soldiers and officers coming from the settlement population and of settlers serving in Area Defense battalions. Indeed, settler and religious soldiers have become the majority in the various army forces responsible for security and policing tasks in the West Bank. All this is reflected in greater pressure exerted on the IDF to adjust itself to the interests, values, and crucially, the goals of that population. However, in the absence of relation work, the competitive nature of this symbiosis can become conflict-laden. In addition to more frequent instances of violence between the sides, the increase in the salience of flanking and polarization in shaping the arena of interaction between the ultra-radical-dominated movement and the IDF gave rise to an ominous development.

This development is still in the making, yet it is possible to outline its main contours. Seeking to bolster their social and political standing, members of the coalition of ultra-radical forces have been capitalizing on the chronically deteriorating security situation on the Israeli–Palestinian front, the Gaza Strip front in particular, and the deepening polarization within Israeli society between Right and Left. Initially, central leaders of the ultra-radical coalition of forces (e.g., Itamar Ben-Gvir, leader of *Otzma Yehudit* [Jewish Power]) were more than ready and willing to take advantage of the rising ethnonational-religious tension and deteriorating security situation. Ongoing rounds of fighting along the Israeli–Gaza Strip border, the deadly "Intifada of the Knives" wave that swept Israel during 2016, and violent clashes on the Temple Mount in the summer of 2017 were used to stress the need for more security and personal safety throughout the country, particularly in the West Bank. In addition to publicly questioning the willingness of the IDF to handle the situation seriously, insinuating at times that it was too soft, even leftwing-oriented, ultra-radical leaders and their grassroots foot soldiers (literally and metaphorically) were quick to act in a variety of ways. This included provocations on the Temple Mount, renewal of Price Tag incidents, and strengthening of Jewish presence in Israeli-Palestinian/Arab neighborhoods and cities. Seen from this perspective, it is not surprising that in the general elections of March 2021 a coalition of ultra-right parties, meaningfully labeled *Ha'Tziyonut Ha'Datit* (Religious Zionism), ran independently of the more moderate and pragmatic political party *Yamina* (Right) and received nearly the same portion of votes.

The fact that together with the Likud and the ultra-orthodox parties, the ultra-radical party remained in the opposition turned out to be no more than a pause. The unprecedentedly short term of the "government of change" (June 2021–June 2022), bringing together pragmatic forces on both the Right and the Left, including an Israeli-Arab party, was marred by a series of national security and defense crises, which began even before it was sworn in. These crises (e.g., another war between Israel and Hamas called operation *Shomer Ha'khomot* [Guardian of the Walls] in May 2021, major confrontations and riots by Israeli-Arab citizens throughout the country in the same month, and a wave of lethal Palestinian terrorism during the spring of 2022) contributed to the further strengthening of the ultra-radical forces and the popularity of their social and political agenda.

In the current Government, as of this writing, the ultra-radical party *Ha'Tziyonut Ha'Datit* is second only to the Likud in terms of power and influence, relying on twice the seats it had in the previous Knesset, with its members Itamar Ben-Gvir, Bezalel Smotrich, and others holding key cabinet positions (e.g., Minister of Finance, a minister in the Defense Ministry, Minister of National Security). Finally in a position to promote their agenda, the conflicting symbiosis between the ultra-radical coalition that nowadays dominates the Settlement Movement and IDF senior officers has become a defining feature of their interaction. What began slowly and hesitantly soon after the government took office gained momentum and took clearer shape following the horrendous Hamas attack on Israel on October 7, 2023, and the ensuing Gaza

War. What leaders of the Ultra-radical coalition seem to be interested in promoting is the broadening of Jewish presence throughout the June 1967 Occupied Territories (including the renewal of Gaza Strip settlements) and their full annexation to the Jewish State of Israel; the strengthening of the Israeli police force and creation of a national guard, both of which would be accountable directly and solely to the Minister of National Security Ben-Gvir, responsible for law and order and internal security in the Greater State of Israel; and the restriction of IDF involvement and responsibilities in defending the Greater State of Israel against external threats.

References

Admoni, Yehiel. 1992. *Decade of Discretion – Settlement Policy in the Territories, 1976–1977*. Ramat Gan: Hakibutz HaMeuchad.

Alimi, Eitan Y. 2018. "'Struggling to Remain Relevant': Why and How Radicalization Was Impeded in the Struggle against the Gaza Pullout." *Canadian Review of Sociology*, 55(4): 597–623.

Alimi, Eitan Y. 2016. "The Relational Context of Radicalization: The Case of Jewish Settler Contention before and after the Gaza Pullout." *Political Studies*, 64(4): 910–929.

Alimi, Eitan Y., and Hirsch-Hoefler, Sivan. 2012. "Structure of Political Opportunities and Threats, and Movement-Countermovement Interaction in Segmented Composite Regimes." *Comparative Politics*, 41: 331–349.

Alimi, Eitan Y., and Maney, Gregory. 2018. "Focusing on Focusing Events: Event Selection, Media Coverage, and the Dynamics of Contentious Meaning-Making." *Sociological Forum*, 33(3): 757–782.

Alimi, Eitan Y., Bosi, Lorenzo, and Demetriou, Chares. 2012. "Relational Dynamics and Processes of Radicalization: A Comparative Framework." *Mobilization*, 17(1): 7–26.

Alimi, Eitan Y., Demetriou, Chares, and Bosi, Lorenzo. 2015. *The Dynamic of Radicalization: A Relational and Comparative Perspective*. New York: Oxford University Press.

Allegra, Marco, and Maggor, Erez. 2022. "The Metropolitanization of Israel's Settlement Policy: The Colonization of the West Bank as a Strategy of Spatial Restructuring." *Political Geography*, 92: 102513. https://doi.org/10.1016/j.polgeo.2021.102513.

Almeida, Paul. 2007. *Waves of Protest – Popular Struggle in El Salvador, 1925–2005*. Minneapolis: University of Minnesota Press.

Aran, Gideon, and Hassner, Ron E. 2013. "Religious Violence in Judaism: Past and Present." *Terrorism and Political Violence*, 25(3): 355–405.

Aran, Gideon. 1985. *Eretz Israel between Politics and Religion: The Movement to Stop the Withdrawal from Sinai*. Jerusalem: Jerusalem Institute for Israel Studies.

Arian, Asher, and Ventura, Rafael. 1989. *Public Opinion in Israel and the Intifada: Changes in Security Attitudes 1987–88*. Tel-Aviv: Jaffee Center for Strategic Studies.

Aronson, Geoffrey. 2008. "Settlement Monitor." *Journal of Palestine Studies*, 37(4): 150–158.

Asal, Victor, and Rethemeyer, Karl R. 2008. "The Nature of the Beast: Organizational Structures and the Lethality of Terrorist Attacks." *Journal of Politics*, 70(2): 437–449.

Ben-Eliezer, Uri. 2012. *Old Conflict, New War: Israel's Politics toward the Palestinians*. New York: Palgrave Macmillan.

Bjørgo, Tore, and John Horgan. (Eds). 2011. *Leaving Terrorism Behind: Individual and Collective Disengagement*. London and New York: Routledge.

Brooke, Nick. 2018. *Terrorism and Nationalism in the United Kingdom: The Absence of Noise*. New York: Palgrave MacMillan.

Burawoy, Michael. 1998. "The Extended Case Method." *Sociological Theory*, 16(1): 4–33.

Busher, Joel, Holbrook, Donald, and Macklin, Graham. 2023. "How the "Internal Brakes' on Violent Escalation Work and Fail: Toward a Conceptual Framework for Understanding Intra-Group Processes of Restraint in Militant Groups." *Studies in Conflict & Terrorism*, 46(10): 1960–1983.

Cochrane, Feargal. 1997. *Unionist Politics and the Politics of Unionism since the Anglo–Irish Agreement*. Cork: Cork University Press.

Cohen, Samy. 2019. *Doves among Hawks: Struggles of the Israeli Peace Movements*. London: Hurst.

Cohen, Stuart A. 1993. "The *Hesder Yeshivot* in Israel: A Church-State Military Arrangement." *Journal of Church and State*, 35(1): 113–130.

Cohen, Stuart A. 1999. "From Integration to Segregation: The Role of Religion in the IDF." *Armed Forces and Society*, 25(3): 387–405.

Collier, Paul, and Hoeffler, Anke. 1999. *Greed and Grievance in Civil War*. Washington, DC: World Bank Policy Research Working Series.

Dalsheim, Joyce. 2011. *Unsettling Gaza: Secular Liberalism, Radical Religion and the Israeli Settlement Project*. New York: Oxford University Press.

De Fazio, Gianluca. 2013. "The Radicalization of Contention in Northern Ireland, 1968–1972: A Relational Perspective." *Mobilization*, 18(4): 475–496.

Della Porta, Donatella. 2013. *Clandestine Political Violence*. Cambridge: Cambridge University Press.

Della Porta, Donatella. 2018. "Radicalization: A Relational Perspective." *Annual Review of Political Science*, 21: 461–474.

Della Porta, Donatella, and LaFree, Gary. 2011. "Processes of Radicalization and De-Radicalization." *International Journal of Conflict and Violence*, 6(1): 4–10.

Della Porta, Donatella, and Reiter, Herbert (Eds.). 1998. *Policing Protest*. Minneapolis: University of Minnesota Press.

Della Porta, Donatella, and Tarrow, Sidney. 1986. "Unwanted Children: Political Violence and the Cycle of Protest in Italy, 1966–1973." *European Journal of Political Research*, 14(5–6): 607–632.

Demant, Peter R. 1988. *Ploughshares into Swords: Israeli Settlement Policy in the Occupied Territories, 1967–1977* (Unpublished Ph.D. Dissertation, Submitted to the University of Amsterdam).

Diani, Mario. 2000. "The Relational Deficit of Ideologically Structured Action." *Mobilization*, 5(1): 17–24.

Diani, Mario. 2003. "Introduction: Social Movements, Contentious Actions, and Social Networks: From Metaphor to Substance?" In Mario Diani and Doug McAdam (eds.), *Social Movements and Networks: Relational Approaches to Collective Action*. Oxford: Oxford University Press, pp. 1–18.

Drevon, Jerome. 2022. *Institutionalizing Violence: Strategies of Jihad in Egypt*. New York: Oxford University Press.

Earl, Jennifer. 2003. "Tanks, Tear Gas, and Taxes: Toward a Theory of Movement Repression." *Sociological Theory*, 21(1): 44–68.

Einwohner, Rachel L. 2007. "Leadership, Authority, and Collective Action: Jewish Resistance in the Ghettos of Warsaw and Vilna." *American Behavioral Scientist*, 50(10): 1306–1326.

Eiran, Ehud, and Krause, Peter. 2016. "Old (Molotov) cocktails in new bottles? 'Price-tag' and settler violence in Israel and the West Bank." *Terrorism and Political Violence*, 30(4): 637–657.

Elliott, Sydney, and Flackes, William D. 1999. *Northern Ireland: A Political Directory, 1968–1999*. Belfast: The Blackstaff Press.

Emigh, Rebecca J. 1997. "The Power of Negative Thinking: The Use of Negative Case Methodology in the Development of Sociological Theory." *Theory and Society*, 26(5): 649–684.

Emirbayer, Mustafa. 1997. "Manifesto for a Relational Sociology." *American Journal of Sociology*, 103(2): 281–317.

Emirbayer, Mustafa, and Mische, Ann. 1998. "What Is Agency?" *American Journal of Sociology*, 103(4): 962–1023.

Feige, Michael. 2009. *Settling in the Hearts – Jewish Fundamentalism in the Occupied Territories*. Detroit: Wayne State University Press.

Feinstein, Yuval. 2022. *Rally 'Round the Flag: The Search for National Honor and Respect in Times of Crisis*. New York: Oxford University Press.

Gazit, Nir. 2015. "State-Sponsored Vigilantism: Jewish Settlers' Violence in the Occupied Palestinian Territories." *Sociology*, 49(3): 438–454.

Gillham, Patrick F., Edwards, Bob, and John A. Noakes. 2013. "Strategic Incapacitation and the Policing of Occupy Wall Street Protests in New York City, 2011." *Policing and Society*, 23(1): 81–102.

Goldstone, Jack. 2004. More Social Movements or Fewer? Beyond Political Opportunity Structures to Relational Fields." *Theory and Society*, 33(3–4): 333–365.

Goodwin, Jeff. 2007. "'The Struggle Made Me a Non-Racialist': Why There Was So Little Terrorism in the Antiapartheid Struggle." *Mobilization* 12(2): 193–203.

Gupta, Dipak K. 2008. *Understanding Terrorism and Political Violence*. London: Routledge.

Haloutz, Dani. 2010. *Straightforward*. Tel Aviv: Miskal.

Harnoy, Meir. 1994. *The Settlers*. Or Yehuda: Ma'ariv book Guild.

Hermann, Tamar. 2009. *The Israeli Peace Movement – A Shattered Dream*. Cambridge: Cambridge University Press.

Hirsch-Hoefler, Sivan, and Mudde, Cas. 2020. *The Israeli Settler Movement – Assessing and Explaining Social Movement Success*. Cambridge: Cambridge University Press.

Huberman, Hagai. 2008. *Against All Odds*. Ariel: Sifriyat Netsarim.

Huberman, Hagai. 2005. *Sources in the Sands*. Nestarim: Netsarim College.

Kaminer, Reuven. 1996. *The Politics of Protest*. Sussex: Sussex Academic Press.

Kimmerling, Baruch. 1979. "Determination of the Boundaries and Frameworks of Conscription: Two Dimensions of Civil-Military Relations in Israel." *Studies in Comparative International Development*, 14(1): 22–41.

Klandermans, Bert. 1988. "The Formation and Mobilization of Consensus." In Bert Klandermans, Hanspeter Kriesi, and Sidney Tarrow (eds.), *From Structure to Action: Comparing Social Movement Research across Cultures*. Greenwich: Blackwell, pp. 173–196.

Kliot, Nurit, and Albeck, Shemuel. 1996. *Sinai – Anatomy of Settlements' Evacuation*. Israel: Ministry of Defense.

Kurtz, Sharon. 2002. *Workplace Justice: Building Multi-Identity Movements*. Minneapolis: University of Minnesota Press.

Levy, Yagil. 2007. "The Embedded Military: Why Did the IDF Perform Effectively in Executing the Disengagement Plan?" *Security Studies*, 16(3): 382–408.

Levy, Yagil. 2014. "The Theocratization of the Israeli Military." *Armed Forces & Society*, 40(2): 269–294.

Lustick, Ian S. 1988. *For the Land and the Lord*. New York: Council on Foreign Relations.

Lustick, Ian S. 1981. "Israel and the West Bank after Eon Moreh: The Mechanics of De Facto Annexation." *The Middle East Journal*, 35(4): 557–577.

Malkki, Leena. 2020. "Learning from the Lack of Political Violence." *Perspectives on Terrorism*, 14(6): 27–36.

McAdam, Doug. 1999. *Political Process and the Development of Black Insurgency, 1930–1970*. Chicago: University of Chicago Press.

McAdam, Doug, and Tarrow, Sidney. 2010. "Ballots and Barricades: The Reciprocal Relations between Elections and Social Movements." *Perspectives on Politics*, 8: 529–542.

McAdam, Doug, Tarrow, Sidney, and Tilly, Charles. 2001. *Dynamics of Contention*. New York: Cambridge University Press.

McCauley, Clark, and Moskalenko, Sophia. 2008. "Mechanisms of Political Radicalization: Pathways toward Terrorism." *Terrorism and Political Violence*, 20(3): 415–433.

McCammon, Holly J. 2003. "'Out of the Parlors and into the Streets': The Changing Tactical Repertoire of the US Women's Suffrage Movements." *Social Forces*, 81(3): 787–818.

Meyer, David S. 2021. *How Social Movements (Sometimes) Matter*. Cambridge: Polity Press.

Meyer, David S., and Tarrow, Sidney (Eds.). 1998. *The Social Movement Society: Contentious Politics for a New Century*. Lanham: Rowman and Littlefield.

Mische, Ann. 2011. "Relational Sociology, Culture, and Agency." In Mario Diani and Doug McAdam (eds.), *Sage Handbook of Social Network Analysis*. London: Sage, pp. 80–97.

Newman, David. 1985. *The Impact of Gush Emunim: Politics and Settlement in the West Bank*. Abingdon: Taylor & Francis.

Pedahzur, Ami. 2012. *The Triumph of Israel's Radical Right*. New York: Oxford University Press.

Pedahzur, Ami, and Perliger, Arie. 2009. *Jewish Terrorism in Israel*. New York: Columbia University Press.

Pedatzur, Reuven. 1996. *The Triumph of Embarrassment*. Tel Aviv: Yad Tabenkin-Galili Research Institute & Bitan.

Peleg, Samuel. 2002. *Zealotry and Vengeance*. Lanham: Lexington Books.

Peri, Yoram. 2006. *Generals in the Cabinet Room: How the Military Shapes Israeli Policy*. Washington, DC: United States Institute of Peace Press.

Piazza, James A. 2006. "Rooted in Poverty? Terrorism, Poor Economic Development, and Social Cleavages." *Terrorism and Political Violence*, 18(1): 159–177.

Roth, Anat. 2005. *The Secret of Its Strength: The Yesha Council and Its Campaign against the Security Fence and the Disengagement Plan*. Jerusalem: Israeli Democracy Institute.

Roth, Anat. 2014. *Not At Any Price – From Gush Katif to Amona*. Tel-Aviv: Miskal.

Rubinstein, Danny. 1982. *On the Lord's Side: Gush Emunim*. Tel Aviv: Hakibbutz Hameuchad.

Segal, Hagai. 1987. *Dear Brothers*. Jerusalem: Keter.

Segal, Hagai. 1999. *Yamit: The End*. Beit-El: Beit-El Publishing House.

Segal. Zeev. 2000. "The Supreme Court of Justice in the Fabric of Israeli Society – Fifty Years Later." *Law and Government*, 5(1): 235–296.

Segev, Tom. 2005. *1967: Israel, the War, and the Year That Transformed the Middle East*. New York: Metropolitan Books.

Shafat, Gershon. 1995. *Gush Emunim: The Backstage Story*. Beit-El: Beit-El Publishing House.

Shifris, Amos. 2013. *The First Rabin Government, 1974–1977*. Tzur Igal: Porat.

Shiloah, Zvi. 1989. *The Guilt of Jerusalem*. Tel Aviv: Zmora-Bitan.

Sprinzak, Ehud. 1991. *The Ascendance of Israel's Radical Right*. New York: Oxford University Press.

Sprinzak, Ehud. 1998. "The Psychological Formation of Extreme Left Terrorism in a Democracy: The Case of the Weathermen." In W. Reich (ed.), *Origins of Terrorism*. Washington, DC: Woodrow Wilson Center Press, pp. 65–85 .

Sprinzak, Ehud. 1999. *Brother against Brother*. New York: The Free Press.

Staggenborg, Suzanne. 1993. "Critical Events and the Mobilization of the Pro-Choice Movement." *Research in Political Sociology*, 6: 319–345.

Steinmo, Sven. 2008. "Historical Institutionalism." In Donatella Della Porta and Michael Keating (eds.), *Approaches and Methodologies in the Social Sciences*. Cambridge: Cambridge University Press, pp. 118–138.

Stern, Jessica. 2003. *Terror in the Name of God: Why Religious Militants Kill*. New York: HarperCollins.

Tamari, Salim. 1981. "The Palestinian Demand for Independence Cannot be Postponed Indefinitely." *MERIP Reports*, 100/101: 28–35.

Taub, Gadi. 2007. *The Settlers – And the Struggle over the Meaning of Zionism*. Tel-Aviv: Miskal.

Tilly, Charles. 2002. *Stories, Identities, and Political Change*. Lanham: Rowman & Littlefield.

Tilly, Charles. 2003. *The Politics of Collective Violence*. Cambridge: Cambridge University Press.

Van Dyke, Nella, and Amos, Bryan. 2017. "Social Movement Coalitions: Formation, Longevity, and Success." *Sociology Compass*, 11(7): 1–17.

Waller, Harold M. 1990. "Israel's Continuing Dilemma." *Current History*, 89-(544): 69–88.

Weisburd, David. 1989. *Jewish Settler Violence*. University Park: The Pennsylvania State University Press.

Weisburd, David, and Lernau, Hagit. 2006. "What Prevented Violence in Jewish Settlements in the Withdrawal from the Gaza Strip?" *Ohio State Journal of Dispute Resolution*, 22(1):37–81.

Wolfsfeld, Gadi. 1988. *The Politics of Provocation: Participation and Protest in Israel*. Albany: State University of New York.

Zertal, Idith, and Eldar, Akiva. 2004. *Lords of the Land: The Settlers and the State of Israel 1967–2004*. Or Yehuda: Kinneret, Zmora-Bitan, Dvir.

Zisser, Baruch, and Cohen, Asher. 1999. "From an Accommodational Democracy to a Democracy in Crisis: The Battle for Collective Identity in Israel." *Politics*, 3: 9–30.

Other Sources

Ehud Sprinzak Interview & Media Collection (located at the library of the Yitzhak Rabin Center, Tel Aviv, Israel)

Davar
Ha'aretz
Ha'tzofe
Ma'ariv
Yediot Achronot

Acknowledgments

This Element began taking shape in 2012 as I was wrapping up a short book on why there was little Jewish settler violence during the struggle against the Gaza Pullout. Already a spirited relationalist yet only partly trained in mechanism-based thinking and analysis, I settled for short historical backgrounds to describe the key features of those structures in which mechanisms operated. Disappointed by the lack of historical perspective and context of that solution, I promised myself to do better. This Element is my belated attempt to follow up on that promise.

Many participated in this journey. A battery of able research assistants, including Alon Burstein, Efrat Daskal, Adi Livni, Hilik Marchek, Perle Nicole, Gaya Polat, Amit Shiniak, and Naama Tridel, made the journey possible and deserve special thanks. The journey also involved many dear colleagues and friends who collaborated on related projects, shared useful thoughts, and offered, sometimes continuously, valuable insights and feedback on previous versions of this Element and other manuscripts on which this Element expands. I am particularly grateful for those coming from Lorenzo Bosi, Chares Demetriou, Gianluca de Fazio, Donatella della Porta, Mario Diani, Sivan Hirsch-Hoefler, Yagil Levi, Ann Mische, Char Ryan, Michael Schwartz, Patricia Steinhoff, Sidney Tarrow, Bob White, and Gilda Zwerman.

During the research conducted for this Element, I received helpful advice and support from Amir Bar-Or, Yaakov Sela, and Avraham Mitzna, for which I am deeply appreciative. Lastly, I thank David Meyer and Suzanne Staggenborg, editors of the Cambridge University Press Element Series, and two anonymous reviewers. The exceptional support and astute feedback I received from David and Suzanne, coupled with the exceptionally useful set of reviews, proved vital in bringing this Element to light.

Cambridge Elements ⁼

Contentious Politics

Elements in the Series

Contested Legitimacy in Ferguson: Nine Hours on Canfield Drive
Joshua Bloom

Contentious Politics in Emergency Critical Junctures: Progressive Social Movements during the Pandemic
Donatella della Porta

Collective Resistance to Neoliberalism
Paul Almeida and Amalia Pérez Martín

Mobilizing for Abortion Rights in Latin America
Mariela Daby and Mason W. Moseley

Black Networks Matter: The Role of Interracial Contact and Social Media in the 2020 Black Lives Matter Protests
Matthew David Simonson, Ray Block Jr, James N. Druckman, Katherine Ognyanova and David M. J. Lazer

Law, Mobilization, and Social Movements: How Many Masters?
Whitney K. Taylor and Sidney Tarrow

Have Repertoire, Will Travel: Nonviolence as Global Contentious Performance
Selina R. Gallo-Cruz

The Anarchist Turn in Twenty-First Century Leftwing Activism
John Markoff, Hillary Lazar, Benjamin S. Case and Daniel P. Burridge

Sixty Years of Visible Protest in the Disability Struggle for Equality, Justice, and Inclusion
David Pettinicchio

Aggrieved Labor Strikes Back: Inter-sectoral Labor Mobility, Conditionality, and Unrest under IMF Programs
Saliha Metinsoy

The Evolution of Authoritarianism and Contentious Action in Russia
Bogdan Mamaev

Relation-Building and Contained Radicalization in the Gaza Pullout Campaign
Eitan Y. Alimi

A full series listing is available at: www.cambridge.org/ECTP